Contents

Introduction: A Philosophy of Teaching

Why Learn Music Theory?
Music theory helps us to understand music and intensifies our appreciation of this moving art form. Music theory helps us to answer questions about music. How does music we love make us feel sorrow, joy or excitement? How do composers create specific effects? How do you arrange and orchestrate music? How can a piece of music be interpreted in different ways to give more depth to performances?

We begin with an understanding of the building blocks and the elements of music. Once we master the fundamentals, we become musically literate, and are able to answer these questions. We can then read musical scores and play an instrument, compose, perform, analyze and interpret music.

Musicians can be successful without being musically literate. Some musicians learn music solely by ear. Musicians also use technology to sidestep musical literacy by creating audio recordings of their musical ideas.

Musical literacy involves two steps – reading notes on a staff and then playing the notes on an instrument. In this class you will learn how to read musical notes on the staff and beginning note identification on a piano keyboard. It is highly recommended that you also learn to read notes on your instrument at the same time. This will keep motivation high (you will be making music!) and make the learning of music literacy more personal and significant.

Musical literacy turns an acoustic or aural form into a visual form and offers many advantages to the musician. Musical ideas can be remembered and repeated even centuries later. When a group of musicians are musically literate, they can discuss musical thoughts using the same language. When trained musicians work from a score, concepts and ideas are clearly and quickly communicated.

Written music can be preserved. Recorded tape and digital media becomes obsolete as the machines that create them are no longer in use. Printed materials last for centuries. Long after a composer is no longer composing, musicians can still play their music. While there are no recordings of the music from 500 years ago, the music can be performed.

Music notation has become a universal language. Musicians in China, Russian, France, the United States, and South America read the same music notation.

Music is an aural time based event – it takes time to listen to music – about the same amount of time every time you listen to the same piece. The process of writing it down transforms music into a visual form that can be learned and studied in different ways. Once we are musically literate we can look at a score and instantly understand a piece of music that takes 5 minutes to perform.

Making a living as a musician can be difficult. We want all the tools available to assist us in our musical endeavors and to ensure our musical success. Learning music notation is a helpful tool to further our musical evolution. Learning musical theory in a structured setting can speed up the process of mastering musical concepts.

How to Learn Music Theory
Music theory must be learned very thoroughly to be helpful in practice. The materials must be learned so well that the musician recognizes them without having to think about it. Some of the materials in the online modules will be taught using short timed tests that must be completed in under a minute. When all of the lessons in the online modules are successfully mastered and the information retained, the material becomes accessible for everyday use and is useful in a musical context.

If music theory is learned only in a superficial manner, it isn't possible to use it in a musical environment. Music theory learned without depth is merely a mathematical exercise and can be quickly forgotten.

When music theory is learned at a deeper level, musical elements such as note reading, key signatures, chords, the order of sharps and flats, and scales become innate knowledge instead of external decoration. This kind of learning starts with memorization, and proceeds to internalization.

These concepts have been used successfully in the classroom for decades. All of the tests and drills are possible to master by average students willing to put in practice time. An online student misses seeing other classmates at the board demonstrating the ability to write out the circle of fifths in under a minute, or spelling all the major triads without thinking. Seeing and hearing the success of other students is very motivating and empowering. The online student must be self-motivated to practice enough to achieve their own success.

Towards this end, regular drills and speed tests on repeated materials are suggested. Learning materials once and going on isn't good enough. Mastering the fundamentals creates an internal knowledge that is essential for a thorough grounding in musical rudiments. Read through each lecture and try all the examples and do all the drills. In all sections there are tips on how to increase your speed in learning the fundamentals. Again this deepens your understanding and helps to internalize the knowledge.

Good luck and happy music making!
Dr. Momilani Ramstrum, San Diego 2011

Chapter One: Staves, Clefs, Notes

I. Staves, notes, stems

Musical notes are single tones and are named after the first 7 notes of the alphabet: A B C D E F G. Music is written on a musical staff. A musical staff is a group of five parallel lines.

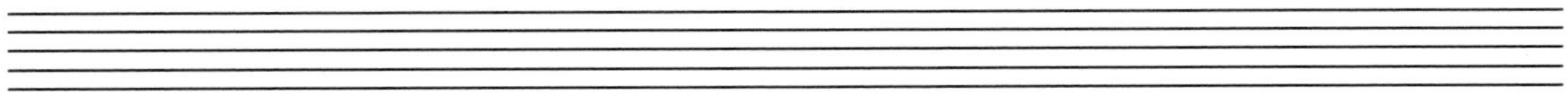

Figure 1.1 The musical staff

Notes are identified by where they sit on the musical staff. Higher pitched notes are higher on the staff and lower notes are lower.

Figure 1.2 Notes on the staff, with higher and lower pitches

Stems

Some notes are hollow oblongs as in Figure 1.2. Other notes are filled in with stems, and others have stems and flags. The variety in appearance of notes indicates the amount of time it takes to play them. The time component of music is called rhythm and will be discussed in later chapters. When a note has a stem on it that goes up, the stem is placed on the right side. When the stem goes down, it is located on the left side. Generally, when a note is below the middle line on the staff, the stem goes up. When a note is above the middle line of the staff the stem goes down. On the middle line, the stem can go in either direction.

Figure 1.3. Notes with stems on the musical staff

II. Treble clef

The clef is shown at the beginning of each system (line) of music notation. The exact pitch of a note is identified by the clef. There are many clefs such as treble, bass, moveable C clefs (alto and tenor clef), octave clef, and percussion clef. We will use the two most common clefs: the treble and the bass clefs.

The treble clef on the musical staff is shown in Figure 1.4.

Figure 1.4 The treble clef

Notice the curl in the middle of the clef that encircles the second line from the bottom. The note G is found on the second line of the staff with a treble clef. For this reason, the treble clef is also called the G clef.

On the musical keyboard there are white notes and black notes. The black notes on the musical keyboard are in groups of two and three. Below the group of two black notes is the note C. The middle-most C on the keyboard is called Middle C. If we count up five notes from Middle C (C, D, E, F, G), we get to the note G. The G on the treble clef and keyboard are located as shown in Figure 1.5.

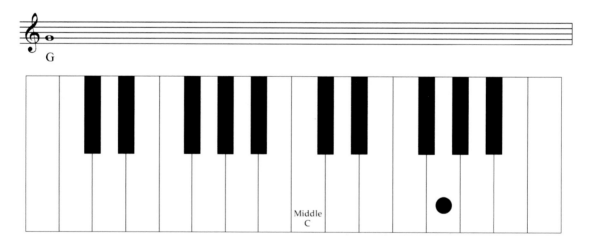

Figure 1.5 The note G on the G clef and keyboard

Practice drawing the treble clef until you can write it easily. When drawing the treble clef, begin by spiraling around the line that is the G note (second from the bottom), then move upward crossing over the second to the top line. Then circle back and draw almost straight downwards, and finish by curving up and backwards.

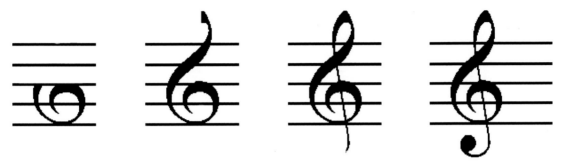

Figure 1.6 Stages of drawing the treble clef

We write notes on every line and space of the musical staff. They are named sequentially, A, B, C, D, E, F, G, A, etc. The note on the space above the note G is A. The note on the next line up is B, then C on the next space, D is on the next line, E is on the next highest space, and F is on the top line.

Figure 1.7. Notes on the treble staff

If we identify just the lines on the treble clef the notes are E G B D F. We can use a sentence to remember these notes: Every Good Boy Does Fine. The notes of the spaces are F A C E.

| E | G | B | D | F | F | A | C | E |
| Every | Good | Boy | Does | Fine | | | | |

Figure 1.8 Treble staff mnemonic

Remembering this sentence is the first step to knowing your notes, though eventually you will know the notes for themselves. Start with the mnemonic sentence or counting lines and spaces up and down from the G note.

III. Bass Clef
The bass clef is the other most commonly used clef. The bass clef is also called the F clef because of the two dots in the clef, above and below the second line from the top, are surrounding the line for the note F. The notes on the lines of the bass clef are G B D F A. We can remember the notes of the bass clef with the mnemonic sentence Good Boys Do Fine Always. The notes on the spaces are A C E G.

Figure 1.9 Bass clef

Practice note identification with the online Note Reading speed drill until you can pass with above 90% accurate and 90% complete. The Note Reading speed drill can be found online at the text website.

Exercise 1.1 Note Reading speed drill – online

IV. Whole steps and half steps on keyboard
The smallest possible distance between each note on the keyboard is called a half step (HS). When there is a black note between two white notes, there is a whole step between the white notes (WS). There is a half step between adjacent white and black notes.

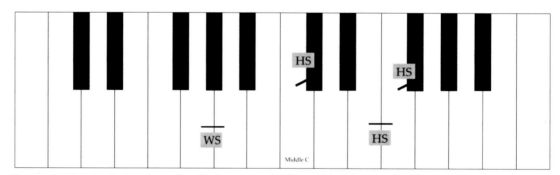

Figure 1.10 Music keyboard: whole steps (WS) and half steps (HS)

C is the white key to the left of the two black keys on the keyboard. D is the next white note to the right. Between the notes C and D there is a whole step because there is a black note in between the two notes. There is no black note between the notes E and F, so the distance is therefore a half step. There is also no black key between the notes B and C, so there is a HS between the notes B and C.

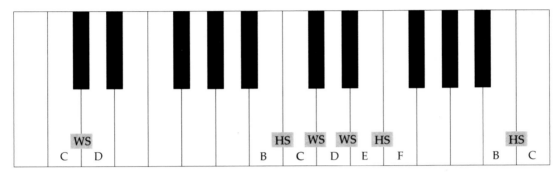

Figure 1.11 The musical keyboard: whole steps and half steps

V. Ledger lines
There are many more notes on the piano than will fit on the treble and bass clefs. These other notes are notated by using ledger lines. You can think of ledger lines as small extensions of the staff lines above and below the main five lines of the staff. The note at the bottom of the treble clef is the note D and below this note is the note C.

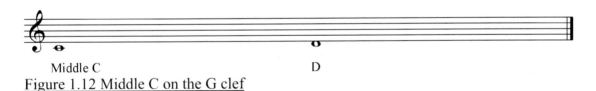

    Middle C   D
Figure 1.12 Middle C on the G clef

Ledger lines are used below and above each clef, usually not more than three ledger lines. Notes using ledger lines on the treble and bass staves are shown in Figures 1.13 and 1.14.

  A   B   C   D   E   C   B   A   G   F
Figure 1.13 Ledger lines above and below the treble staff

| C | D | E | F | G | E | D | C | B | A |

Figure 1.14 Ledger lines above and below bass clef

Practice the note identification Note Reading speed drill with ledger lines until you can pass with above 90% accuracy and completion. The ledger line Note Reading speed drill can be found online at the text website.

Exercise 1.2 Ledger line Note Reading speed drill – online

VI. Pitch octave designation

On a full size piano there are eight Cs. The fourth C, up from the lowest pitch, is the middle most C on the keyboard. This note is Middle C and is also called C4. (C is the pitch, the 4 is the octave designation). Put together, C4, is called the pitch octave designation and identifies which of the 8 possible Cs we want to play.

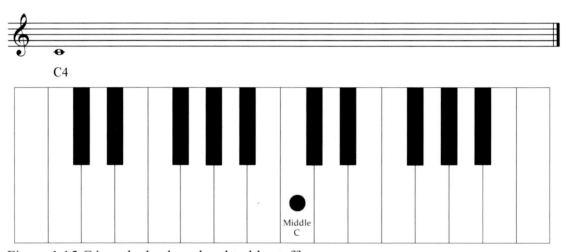

Figure 1.15 C4 on the keyboard and treble staff

All of the notes above the note C4 until the next C are also designated with number 4, D4 E4, etc. The pitch octave number always references the octave number of the C below the note. For example B4 is the B above middle C, just below C5 as shown in Figure 1.16.

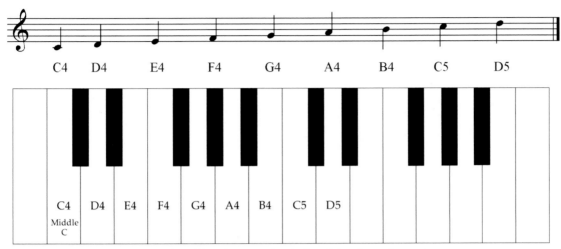

Figure 1.16 Pitch octave identification on G clef and keyboard

On the bass clef C3 is located on the second space from the bottom.

C3   D3   E3   F3   G3   A3   B3   C4   D4

Figure 1.16a Pitch octave identification on F clef

What is the pitch octave designation?

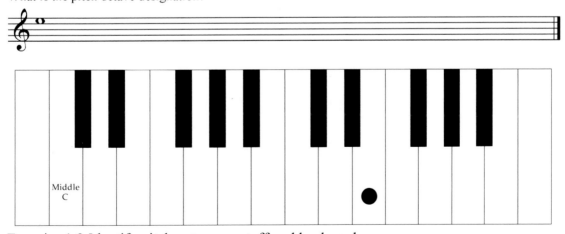

Exercise 1.3 Identify pitch octave on staff and keyboard

The same notes can be written in different clefs using ledger lines. The note F3 can be written in the G clef (treble clef) with three ledger lines below the staff. Or D4 can be written on the F clef (bass clef) above the first ledger line, as shown in Figure 1.17. Which clef is used depends on what instrument will play the note or how the note will be played.

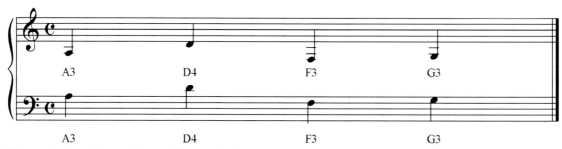

Figure 1.17 F4 in treble and bass clefs.

A classical guitarist only reads music in the treble clef so the note E3, the lowest note on the guitar will be written in the treble clef. The same note E3 will usually be notated in the bass clef for the piano, indicating that the note should be played with the left hand.

Exercise 1.4 Identify pitch octave of the notes in different clefs

VII. Accidentals, naturals
Notes can be changed by a half step through the use of accidentals. Accidentals are placed before the note on the staff, on the same line or space as the note they modify. The accidentals are ♯ ♭ × ♭♭ and ♮ (sharp, flat, double sharp, double flat, and natural).

Sharp (♯) raises the note by a half step. Flat (♭) lowers the pitch by a half step. Double sharp (×) raises the note by two half steps. Double flat (♭♭) lowers the note by two half steps. A natural sign (♮) cancels out other accidentals.

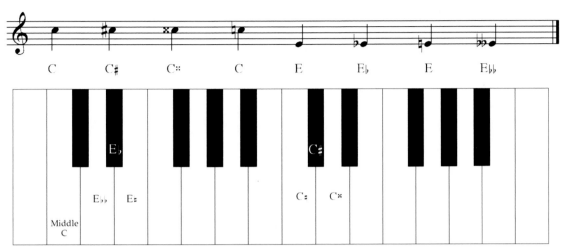

Figure 1.18 Accidentals on the treble staff and keyboard

Accidentals are written in music on the left side of the note. This allows the musician who is reading the notation to know that the note has an accidental before they play the note. However when written as text, accidentals are placed to the right of the note, following how we would speak the name of the note: C♯ - C sharp.

Identify these notes

Exercise 1.5 Identify notes with accidentals

VIII. Enharmonic notes
Enharmonic notes are notes that sound the same but have different names. The black keys on the piano all have two names. For example the note a half step above C is named both C♯ or D♭. C♯ and D♭ are called enharmonic equivalents.

All notes can be named enharmonically. The note E can also be called F♭ and C can be renamed enharmonically as B♯. The reason to name a note E versus F♭ has to do with what scale is being used. The notes E and F♭ are enharmonic equivalents; on the piano they sound the same.

Figure 1.19 Enharmonic notes E and F♭

The note G can also be called A♭♭ (2 HS below A). E✕ is 2 HS above the note E and is enharmonic to the notes F♯ and G♭.

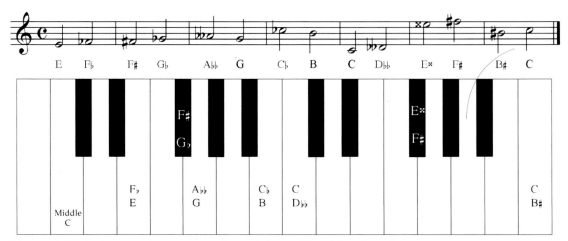

Figure 1.20 Enharmonic notes on the treble staff and keyboard

Name the note, then notate and name two enharmonic notes for the given note

Exercise 1.6 Enharmonic notes

IX. The Grand Staff
When the treble and bass clefs are shown together with a brace to the left, this is called the grand staff. This is used for notating piano music.

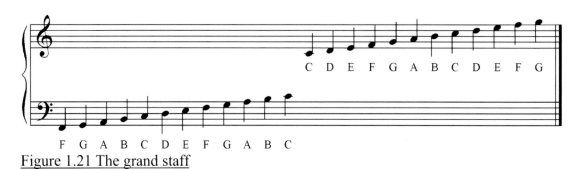

Figure 1.21 The grand staff

Middle C is notated closer to the treble or bass clef to indicate which hand will play the note.

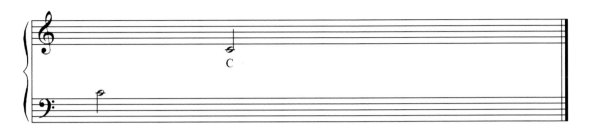

Figure 1.22 Middle C in treble and bass clefs

Practice the the treble, bass, and ledger line Note Reading speed drills online. Speed is necessary to acquire immediacy of pitch identification. Practice note identification Note Reading speed drills until you can pass above 90% accurate and 90% complete. The Note Reading speed drills can be found online at the text website.

Exercise 1.7 Speed drills for both clefs – online

X. Common Notation Errors
Today, most professional musicians use music notation software. However all scores should look professional, even when writing music notation by hand. Here are common errors that beginners make and how to avoid them.

Incorrect	Correct
Notes and stems look like lollipops	Stems are not centered on the bottom or top of note, they are on the right if the stem goes up, and on the left if the stem goes down.
Notes are drawn like round circles.	Notes are actually tilted ovals, not circles.
Note stems are falling over to right or left.	Note stems should be completely vertical.
Accidentals are small and tiny in comparison to the notehead	The accidental is as important as the note. It should be as big as the note with the vertical stem of the flat sign about as high as the stem of the note.
Stems are too short	Stems on notes extend from the note to about 3 staff lines up or down.
Stems are on the wrong side of the note.	Stems are on the right if the stem goes up, and on the left if the stem goes down.
Accidentals are on a different line or space than the note they modify.	Accidentals must be on the exact same line or space as the note they modify.
Accidentals are put after the note they modify.	Accidentals are written before the note in music notation, but are written after the note when writing text.

The vertical lines are tilted and the horizontal lines are straight on the sharp sign.	The vertical lines should be straight up and down on the sharp sign. The horizontal lines however have an upward tilt.
For the flat sign, it looks like the letter b.	The flat sign comes to a point, like half a heart, at the bottom of the sign.
Quarter notes are written with big circles, then colored in, taking 30 seconds per note to draw.	When writing notes by hand, a few lines at an angle are sufficient to delineate a note. Don't spend a lot of time and ink on each note.
Ledger lines are written on both sides of the note.	Notes need ledger lines only on one side. For example the note B3 on the treble staff (just below middle C), should only have a ledger line above it. It is incorrect to put a ledger line on either side of it.
Notes are ambiguous in pitch and cover more than one line or space.	Notes should be written precisely, covering only one line or space.

Figure 1.23 Common notation errors

Homework 1

I. Draw 5 treble clefs.　　　　　　　　II. Draw 5 bass clefs.

III. Draw and label 10 notes in the treble staff with stems up.

IV. Draw and label 10 notes in the bass staff with stems down.

V. Draw and label 10 notes in the treble staff using all the accidentals. (♯, ♭, 𝄪, ♭♭, ♮)

VI. Enter B♭4 on the staff and keyboard.

VII. Enter E♯2 on the staff and keyboard.

VIII. Enter A𝄪4, E♭5, C♭♭6, and G𝄪5 on the staff and key board.

IX. Enter G♯3, B♭3, A𝄪2, and C♭3 on the staff and keyboard.

X. Identify the notes and label whole steps or half steps.

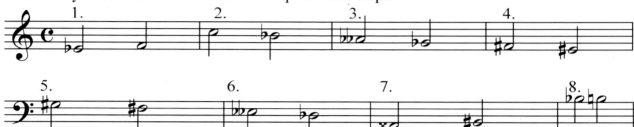

XI. Notate and identify the enharmonic equivalents.

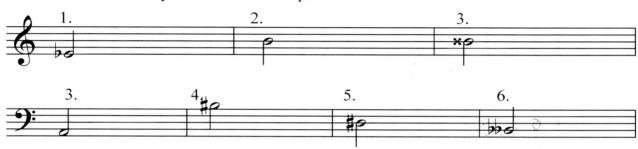

XII. Identify the notes and pitch octave (e.g. middle C is C4)

XIII. Identify whole steps and half steps.

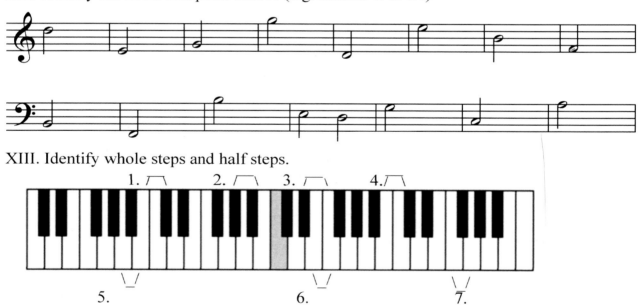

XIV. Indicate where each note on the staff is located on the keyboard

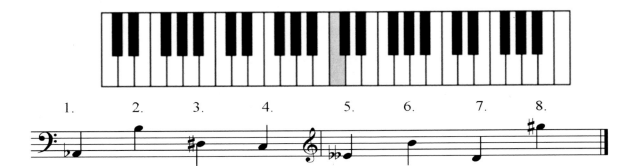

Homework 2

I. Identify the pitch including the pitch octave number, then rewrite the given pitch in the other clef. Number 1 is done for you.

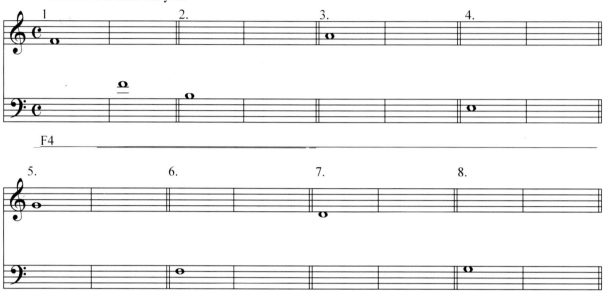

F4

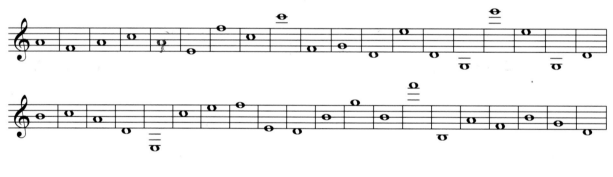

II. Identify pitch and pitch octave.

Chapter Two: Simple Rhythm

I. Rhythm, beats, meter and accents

Rhythm, a fundamental element of music, is a recurring pattern of duration and accent. The study of rhythm can be very complex. In any discussion of rhythm we must first understand the difference between rhythm, beat, meter and accent.

In Figure 2.1, the example begins with four regular pulses in the bass clef. This is the beat. The pulse continues while a more complicated phrase is played in the treble clef. This is the rhythm. The loudest sounds are heard every four beats (indicated by the > above the notes). This is an accent. The accents are repeated every 4 beats, which defines the meter. The meter in this example is in 4.

Figure 2.1 Beat and rhythm.

Why do we care about meter? Meter is about accents. If music had no accents it would be lifeless and uninteresting.

II. Simple meter and bar lines

We determine meter by the recurring accents. Accents every 2 and 4 beats are the most common in today's music. When each beat is subdivided into groups of two and four, this is called simple meter. Simple meter can also have accents every 3 beats. Notes are grouped on the staff into measures, divided by vertical lines called bar lines. The strongest beat occurs most often on beat 1, the first note after the barline.

In Figure 2.2 notice the accents occur every two beats. In Figure 2.3 the accents occur every three beats. In Exercise 2.1 how often do accents occur?

Figure 2.2 Meter in 2

Figure 2.3 Meter in 3

Is the meter in groups of 2, 3, or 4?

Exercise 2.1 What is the meter? How often do accents occur?

III. Notes and time values

Notes are assigned time values and are identified by their appearance (filled in or hollow, stem or flag). Below are the most commonly used time values for notes. Notice the whole note has no stem, while all the other notes have stems. The whole note and the half note are hollow while the rest of the note heads are filled in. The eighth note and sixteenth notes have flags on their stems.

Notes and counts

whole note | 4 counts | ○
half note | 2 counts | ♩
quarter note | 1 count | ♩
eighth note | 1/2 count | ♪
sixteenth note | 1/4 count | ♪

The notes are proportional. If we assign a note value of one beat for the quarter note, then the half notes get double, or 2 beats, the whole note gets double the value of the half note or 4 beats. There are also notes with shorter durations. The eighth note gets half the value of the quarter note, or 1/2 beat. The sixteenth note gets half the rhythmic value of the eighth note, or 1/4 beat.

Figure 2.4 Whole notes, half notes, quarter notes, eighth notes, sixteenth notes beat values

When notes have flags, they are grouped together with beams.

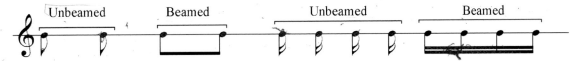

Figure 2.5 Unbeamed and beamed notes

Each note value has an equivalent rest. A rest is a silent space holder in music. Rests are as important as the notes.

Rests, equivalent notes and counts
whole note | 4 counts | o | whole rest | ▬
half note | 2 counts | ♩ | half rest | ▬
quarter note | 1 count | ♩ | quarter rest | 𝄽
eighth note | 1/2 count | ♪ | eighth rest | 𝄾
sixteenth note | 1/4 count | ♬ | sixteenth rest | 𝄿

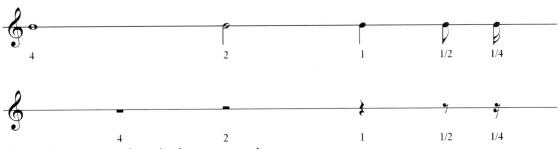

Figure 2.6 Notes and equivalent rests and counts

In the most common meter the quarter note equals one beat. However if the eighth note equals one beat, the quarter note gets two beats, the half note gets four beats, the sixteenth note equals 1/2 beat.

IV. How to make one beat
Twenty five cents, fifty cents, add up to $1.
If we assign a quarter note to get one beat, the sixteenth note gets 1/4 of the beat. We can think of the sixteenth notes as having a value of 25 cents – one quarter of a beat or 1/4 of a dollar. Four sixteenth notes have the same value as one quarter note - that is four 25 cents equal $1. Another way of saying this is four 1/4 beats, or 4 sixteenth notes equal one beat.

1   =   25cents +   25cents +   25cents   +   25cents

Figure 2.7 Four sixteenth notes equal one beat

There are many ways of making one beat: four sixteenth notes, two sixteenth notes plus one eighth note, or one quarter note. If we choose two sixteenth notes and one eighth note, they can be in any order.

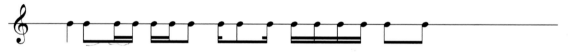

Figure 2.8 Ways to make a beat

What are groups of one beat?

Exercise 2.2 Create one beat. If quarter note gets the beat, pick out groups of one beat.

V. Stem direction
When a note has a stem on it that goes up, the stem is on the right side. When the stem goes down it is located on the left side. Generally when a note is below the middle line on the staff, the stem goes up. When it is located above the middle line the stem goes down. On the middle line, the stem can go in either direction.

Figure 2.9 Stem direction with note placement on staff

VI. Time Signatures

A time signature has two numbers, one on top of another such as ⁴⁄₄. It isn't a fraction - when you write it, don't put a line between the two numbers. Just write two numbers stacked on top of one another.

The time signature is found at the beginning of a piece of music or when the meter changes. There are two numbers that identify the meter. The top number in simple meter identifies how many beats occur before the next accented beat. The bottom number tells what note gets the beat.

If a 4 is on the bottom the quarter note gets one beat, the half note two beats, the whole note four beats, the eighth note a half a beat, and the sixteenth note gets a quarter of a beat.

Figure 2.10 Time signature: ⁴⁄₄ and beats

If the top number is 4 and the bottom number is 4, there are four beats in a measure and the quarter note gets one beat.

If the top number is 4 and the bottom number is 8, there are 4 beats per measure and the eighth note gets one beat.

Figure 2.11 Time signature of ⁴⁄₈. How many beats does each note get?

The numbers on the bottom are always multiples of 2. The top number can be any number but commonly is 2, 3, or most often 4.

The time signature ⁴⁄₄ is also called common time and the time signature is sometimes shown as a C. This is a historical symbol that contrasts with the time signature for ³⁄₄ which was symbolized by a circle. Historically, meters in 3 were considered perfect like the circle.

What gets the beat?

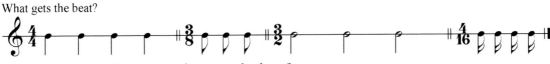

Exercise 2.3 Simple meter, what gets the beat?

How many beats?

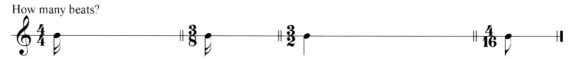

Exercise 2.4 Simple meter, how many beats does each note get?

VII. Beaming by the beat and counting

Some notes such as eighth notes and sixteenth notes can be put together with beams to form beat groups. Beams are the horizontal lines that connect notes that have flags such as eighth notes and sixteenth notes. Eighth notes have one flag when unbeamed and one horizontal line when they are beamed together. Sixteenth notes have two flags when unbeamed and two horizontal lines when beamed together.

Figure 2.12 Beat groups of eighths and sixteenths in ⁴⁄₄ time

We always beam notes by the beat. This means we beam notes together that create one beat. How do we beam? By the beat.

How do we know when a group of notes should be beamed? We add together the fraction of a beat for each note, from left to right until we get to one beat. Then beam those notes together. To figure this out we write in the number of beats or fraction of a beat under every note. Then we write in the count. Notes that get half a beat such as two eighth notes in ²⁄₄ meter, will be counted '1 &' (pronounced one and). They form one beat and are beamed together

Figure 2.13 Four eighth notes in ²⁄₄ meter with counts

Four sixteenth notes each get 1/4 of the beat and are counted as '1 e & a' (pronounced one – ee – and – uh)

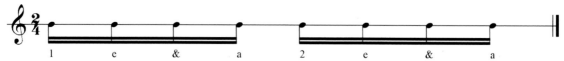

Figure 2.14 Eight sixteenth notes in ²⁄₄ meter with counts

You can mix up the sixteenth and eighth notes in one beat by using 2 sixteenths and 1 eighth in any combination. Think of it as a sixteenth note is worth 25 cents. You can have 4 quarters in a $1 (four sixteenth notes in one beat), or 2 quarters and a 50 cent piece to add up to $1 (two sixteenth notes and one eighth note).

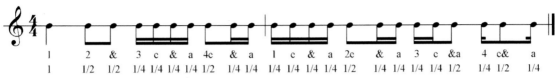

Figure 2.15 Different combinations of eighth and sixteenth notes with counts and beats

If you have difficulty with counting notes and beats, follow the following steps:
1. What gets the beat?
2. How much of the beat does each note get? Under each note write the part of the beat or number of beats.
3. Write in the counts; remember to always write all the numbers even if there are rests. Start over at 1 after every bar line.
4. There must be a count under every note or rest.
5. Count from one to the number of beats in every measure. Don't skip numbers as every whole number (1, 2, 3, 4, etc.) must be written in. For fractions of beats, if there is no note you don't have to write in a count (you don't have to write '&' for example between quarter notes if there are no eighth notes).

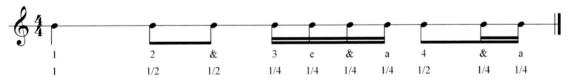

Figure 2.16 ⁴⁄₄ meter with sixteenths, eighths, quarter, half notes: number of beats and counts

When you get good at rhythms, you can write in the counts directly. If this is new to you or you are having difficulty, start by writing in the amount of beats each note gets. Follow the same procedure if you use a mixture of notes and rests.

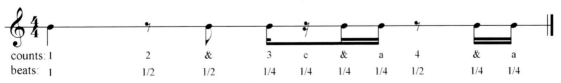

Figure 2.17 How many beats and counts in ⁴⁄₄ meter

How many beats?

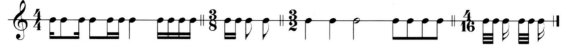

Exercise 2.5 Write in how many beats for each note? Write in counts below.

When music is not beamed properly it is difficult to read. When beaming you must show the beat. How do we beam? By the beat. The first measure in Figure 2.18 is more difficult to read because the notes are not beamed at all.

Figure 2.18 Eighth and sixteenth notes unbeamed and beamed.

In the first measure in Figure 2.19 the notes are beamed incorrectly and are also difficult to sight-read. In the second measure the beaming is corrected.

Figure 2.19 Eighth and sixteenth notes are beamed incorrectly then beamed correctly

Beam the notes.

Exercise 2.6 Beam the following notes in the given time signatures.

VIII. Meter classification

Meter is classified using two general terms; for example 'simple quadruple.' The first term, simple, describes the type of meter that we have examined in this chapter. When we say that the meter is simple, it means that the bottom number in the time signature gets the beat, and the subdivisions of the beat will normally be in groups of 2 or 4. The second term in meter classification (quadruple, duple, or triple) tells us how many beats are in a measure. In simple quadruple meter the bottom number gets the beat and there are four beats in a measure. Some examples of simple quadruple meter are $\frac{4}{4}$, $\frac{4}{8}$, and $\frac{4}{16}$. Music written in any of these three meters can sound exactly the same. Simple triple meter has three beats per measure. Some examples of simple triple meter are $\frac{3}{8}$, $\frac{3}{4}$, and $\frac{3}{16}$. In simple duple there are two beats per measure. Some examples of simple duple meter are

$\frac{2}{4}$ and $\frac{2}{2}$. The other general type of meter besides simple meter is compound meter. We will examine compound meter in Chapter Four.

Why use meter classification? Meter classification tells us about the sound of a piece of music. Music with the same meter classification can sound similar even though it might look very different on paper. A piece of music can be written in $\frac{4}{4}$ or $\frac{4}{16}$ can sound exactly the same though notated differently. Figure 2.20 is a short example notated in $\frac{4}{4}$ and then in $\frac{4}{8}$. Although the note values look different, the sound is exactly the same,

Figure 2.20 Four measures in $\frac{4}{4}$ and $\frac{4}{16}$

What is the meter classification?

Exercise 2.7 What is the meter classifications?

IX. Ties and dots
Ties

When two notes on the same pitch are connected by a curved line, this is called a tie and indicates that the first note is held for the rhythmic value of both notes.

Figure 2.21 Tied notes

Dots

When a dot is placed to the right of the note it extends the rhythmic value of the note by half of the rhythmic value of the note.

A half note (♩) in ⁴⁄₄ time signature gets 2 counts. A dotted half (♩.) note gets 3 counts: 2 counts of the half note + half of the two counts or 1 count = 3 counts total.

|12|3|4|123|4|

Figure 2.22 Notes with dots and ties

Write in the counts.

Exercises 2.8 Write in the counts

Homework 3

I. In the given time signature, how many beats are shown? The measures might not be complete.

II. What is the top number in the time signature if each problem is one complete measure.

III. Beam the notes correctly in each time signature. Write in the counts.

IV. In the time signature, add bar lines. If the final measure is complete, add the final barline.
Write in the counts.

Homework 4

I. How many beats in each problem. Some measures are not complete. Write in the counts.

Counts _____

Beats _____   _____   _____   _____

Counts _____

Beats _____   _____   _____   _____

II. Rewrite the notes and beam corrrectly in the given meter. Write in the counts.

Counts _____

Counts _____

III. Insert barlines. If the final measure is complete, put in the final barline. Write in the counts.

Counts _____

Counts _____

IV. What is the top number in the time signature if this is one measure? Write in the counts.

Counts _____

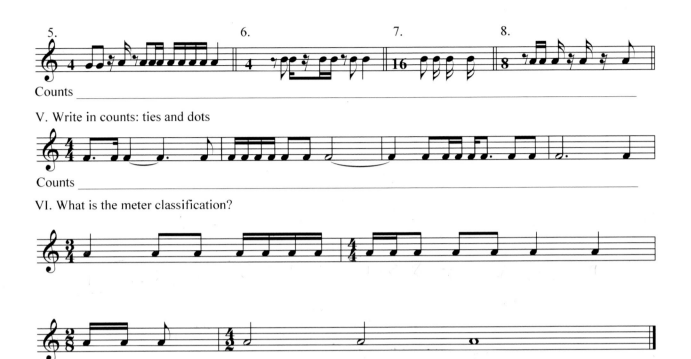

Counts _____

V. Write in counts: ties and dots

Counts _____

VI. What is the meter classification?

Chapter Three: Musical Directions

I. The Italian Language for Musical Directions
Musical terms for dynamics (loud or soft), tempo (fast or slow), mood, form, sections and repetitions are written in Italian. Why Italian? Italy was a center for artist developments during the 1500s, the time of the Renaissance. Much of music notation was formalized at this time in Italy. In the 19th century there were nationalistic movements in Europe and many composers wrote musical directions in their native languages. As music was circulated to other countries difficulties arose in understanding how the music was to be performed. In the twentieth century the majority of composers began to write directions in Italian again, making for greater clarity across national boundaries.

II. Musical Directions
Repeat Sign
Music can be written more concisely by using directions for exact repetitions. A section can be repeated by using the repeat sign instead of writing out the section twice. Repeat signs usually come in mirrored pairs.

Figure 3.1 A pair of repeat signs

A repeat sign tells the performer to go back to the other side of the repeat sign. If there is no other side to the repeat sign, it indicates to play from the beginning.

Figure 3.2 The repeat sign in a score

Da Capo al Fine

Musical directions can be more complex. When *Da Capo al Fine* (abbreviated as *D. C. al Fine*) is marked in the score, the performer repeats from the beginning and plays to the marked end. *Da Capo al Fine* is Italian for 'from the head to the end.' When *Fine* is found in the middle of the score along with a double bar line, it indicates the marked ending.

There is a simple example with *D. C. al Fine* in Figure 3.3. The piece is first played from measure 1 to measure 7. Then the performer returns to the beginning, measure 1, and plays to measure 5 where *Fine* is marked in the score and there is a final double bar line.

Figure 3.3 *D.C al Fine* in a score

Dal segno al fine

Dal segno al fine (abbreviated *D.S. al Fine*) means 'from the sign to the end' and indicates that the performer must go back to where the sign is found in the score and play until the end, which is marked in the score by the word *Fine* and a double bar.

In Figure 3.4 the piece is performed from the beginning to where *D.S. al Fine* is marked in the score at measure 7. Then the performer searches for the *segno*, the sign in the score, found at measure 3. The performer then plays from measure 3 to the end marked by *Fine* and a double bar (measure 5).

Figure 3.4 Musical example with *D.S. al Fine*

First and second endings

First and second endings are shown below Figure 3.5. The first time the piece is played, the first ending is performed. Then the player returns either to the beginning or the other side of the repeat sign. The second time the piece is played, the first ending is skipped and the second ending is played. In Figure 3.5 the example is played from measure 1 to measure 4, the first ending. The player returns to the beginning, measure 1, and plays to measure 3, skips measure 4, and ends with measure 5.

Figure 3.5 Musical example with first and second endings

III. Dynamics

Dynamics indicate how loudly or softly the composer wants a section of a piece of music played. These directions are abbreviations of Italian words and are marked in the score where the dynamics change. Here is a list of dynamic markings in the score and what they are called and how they should be performed. Dynamics are always relative and it is left to the performer how they should be interpreted.

Abbreviation	Italian	Meaning
fff	fortississimo	Loudest possible
ff	fortissimo	Very loud
f	forte	Loud
mf	mezzo forte	Moderately loud
mp	mezzo piano	Moderately soft
p	piano	Soft
pp	pianissimo	Very soft
ppp	pianississimo	Softest possible

Here are some other Italian words that give directions on how to interpret music.

Abbreviation or symbol	Italian	Meaning
sfz	sforzando	Suddenly loud
pf	pianoforte	Soft then loud
fp	fortepiano	Loud then suddenly soft
< or cresc.	crescendo	Gradually louder
> or descresc. or dim.	descrescendo diminuendo	Gradually softer
rit.	ritardando	Gradually slow down
accel.	accelerando	Gradually get faster
a tempo	a tempo	To original tempo

Dynamics are shown in a musical context in Figure 3.6. The piece begins very softly, *pianissimo*. At measure 3 the dynamics get gradually louder until measure 5 where they are *fortissimo*, very loud. Measures 6 and 7 are played moderately loudly, *mezzo forte*. The piece begins again at measure 1 with the same dynamics and ends at measure 5.

Figure 3.6 Example of music with dynamic markings

IV. Metronome markings and tempo directions

Since the invention of the metronome in the 1800s, most scores indicate tempo directions by the number of beats/minute. For example ♩ = 60 means that the piece is played at the rate of 60 quarter notes per minute or one quarter note every second. In addition to the metronome marking, there is often a descriptive term about the tempo. Before metronomes these descriptive terms were the only indication of tempo. Meter is independent of tempo.

Italian term	Meaning
Adagio	slowly
Allegretto	Moderately fast
Allegro	Fast, lively
Andante	Walking pace, moderately fast
Largo	Broadly, slowly
Moderato	Moderately
Presto	Very quickly
Vivace	Very lively

In Figure 3.7 the example has added tempo markings. The piece begins slowly, *Adagio*, then speeds up to a lively, fast tempo (*Allegro*) in the second section. The marking *D.C. al Fine* indicates that the performer returns to the beginning and play *Adagio* (slowly) until the *Fine* (marked end) at measure 5.

Figure 3.7 Tempo markings in a musical example

V. Octave sign

The octave sign is used if the music is to be played an octave higher or lower than written. If the music in Figure 3.8 is written as in the first system, it is difficult to sight read due to all the ledger lines. In the second system it is notated for ease of reading with no ledger lines, using the octave sign. The *8vb* and the dashed line below the staff indicates that the phrase is to be played an octave lower than written. The third system has no octave sign and would be played an octave above the first and second systems.

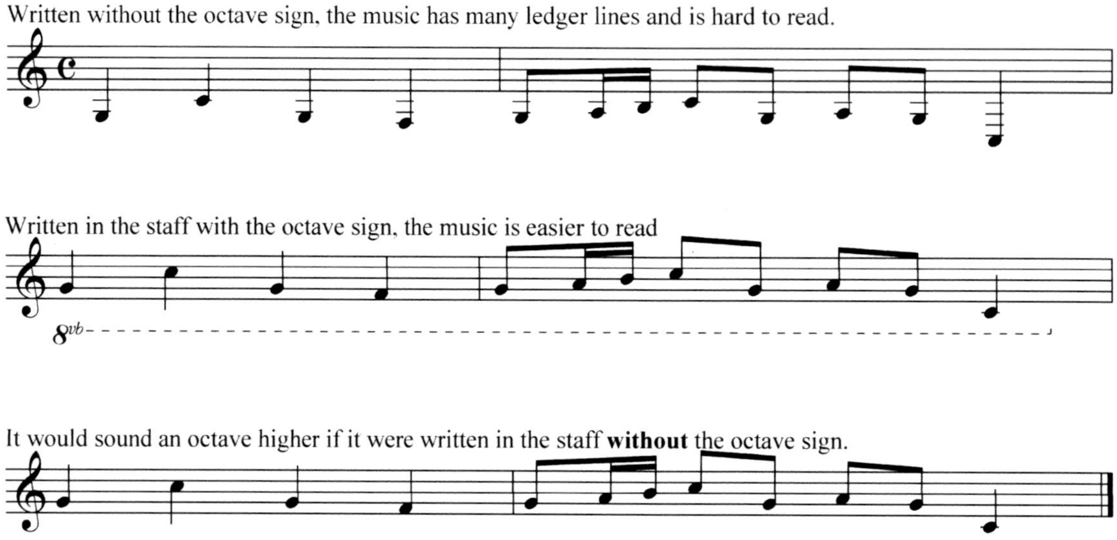

Written without the octave sign, the music has many ledger lines and is hard to read.

Written in the staff with the octave sign, the music is easier to read

It would sound an octave higher if it were written in the staff **without** the octave sign.

Figure 3.8 The octave sign

When the octave sign is used, the notes can be placed within the musical staff for ease of reading, but are played an octave higher or lower. The octave sign can vary: it can be displayed as 8, 8va, 8vb. However 8vb is only used for lowering the pitch an octave. For a two octave change of pitch, use 15ma. The process of changing one note (or more) to another pitch by a fixed amount, is called transposition. When a note or musical phrase is changed by an octave using the octave sign, it has been transposed by one octave.

Musicians generally prefer to read music without ledger lines wherever possible. In Figure 3.8 the music in the first line has ledger lines on every note making the music more difficult to read. On the second line of Figure 3.8, the music is notated an octave higher, within the staff and uses no ledger lines. The octave sign *below* the staff indicates the music is played an octave lower. The last line in Figure 3.8 (a line of music is called a system) shows the music without the octave sign; the third system of music is played an octave higher than the first two lines of music in Figure 3.8. In the first two systems the starting note is G3 and the ending note is C3. In the last system of music, the starting note is G4 and the ending note is C4 – an octave higher.

If the music is to be played an octave higher as in Figure 3.9, the octave sign is written above the staff. In Figure 3.9 the first measure shows how the music might appear in a score. The second measure shows how it would actually be played. If the music was written an octave lower without the octave sign, as in the third measure, it would sound an octave lower.

Written   Played   Sounds octave lower without octava

Figure 3.9 Octave sign and transposition

The octave sign can be used above or below any clef to indicate the music is actually played an octave higher (the octave sign is above the staff) or lower (the octave sign is below the staff).

What is the pitch octave designation for each note?

Exercise 3.1 Phrase with octave sign, Write in pitch octave designation

Rewrite without ledger lines using the octave sign

Exercise 3.2 Phrase with ledger lines, rewrite with octave sign.

Rewrite in other staff using the octave sign

Exercise 3.3 Notes with octave sign. Rewrite the same pitch in other staff

Homework 5

I. Identify the pitch octave and then rewrite the note in the opposite clef using an octave sign.

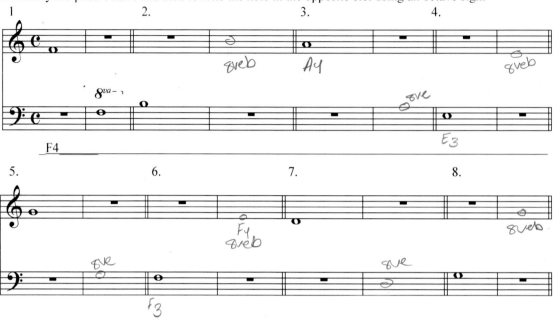

II. Rewrite the notes in the same clef below using the octave sign

III. Identify the notes and pitch octave. e. g. C4.

IV. Define the following words including where you would see these terms in a musical score:

1. *Largo*

2. *Decrescendo*

3. *Ritardando*

4. *Moderato*

5. *Fortissimo*

6. *D.C. al Fine*

7. *Presto*

8. *Piano*

9. *Pianissimo*

10. *Forte*

11. *Mezzo Forte*

12. *A tempo*

13. Transposition

14. *Adagio*

15. Tempo

16. Meter

17. Beat

V. How do you write the following terms in a musical score? What do they tell the performer to do?

1. Repeat sign

2. *Mezzo piano*

3. *Dal segno al fine*

4. *Octave* sign

5. *crescendo*

Chapter Four: Compound Rhythm

I. Is the meter simple or compound?

In Chapter Two we discussed simple meter in which musical beats are usually divided into 2 or 4 parts. There is another type of meter, called compound meter, which divides the beat into three parts. To determine if a time signature is simple or compound we look at the top number of the time signature. If the top number of the time signature is divisible by three but not three, it is compound meter.

Figure 4.1 Examples of compound meter

All examples in Figure 4.1 are compound meter. The top numbers of the time signature, the numbers 6, 9, and 12 are all divisible by 3 but not 3.

Simple or compound?

Exercise 4.1 Simple or compound meter?

II. How many beats in a measure?

In simple meter the top number of the time signature is the number of beats per measure. In $\frac{4}{4}$ meter (simple quadruple meter) there are four beats per measure. To find the number of beats per measure in compound meter, divide the top number by three. If the meter is $\frac{6}{8}$ the top number is 6, so it is compound meter and there are two beats per measure.

If the meter is $\frac{6}{8}$, 6/3 = 2, there are two beats per measure.

6/3 = 2 beats   9/3 = 3 beats   12/3 = 4 beats

Figure 4.2 Compound meter and beats per measure.

How many beats per measure?

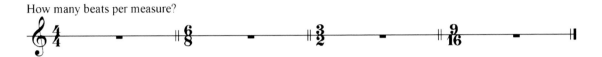

Exercise 4.2 How many beats per measure? Simple and compound meter.

III. Why do we care about meter and what gets the beat?

Meter is about accents. If we spoke or played music with no accents, it would be very dull. Music comes alive when it is played using accents. Accents based on meter are called metric accents. Knowing the meter gives us a pattern for the metric accents. The strongest accent in a measure is usually on the first beat, the downbeat. Sometimes there are secondary accents in a measure. In ⁴₄ meter the primary accent is on one, the secondary accent is on the third beat. In ⁶₈ meter the primary accent is on the first beat and a secondary accent on the second beat if you are counting to 2 and on count 4 if you are counting to 6. We'll discuss counting in compound rhythm below.

Figure 4.3 In ⁶₈ meter the primary accent and secondary accents

IV. What gets the beat?
Simple Meter

In simple meter, the bottom number gets the beat. In ⁴₄ meter, the 4 is on the bottom, so the quarter note gets the beat. In ⁴₂ meter, the half note gets the beat and in ⁴₈ meter the eighth note gets the beat.

Simple Rhythm: What gets the beat?

Quarter note   Eighth note   Sixteenth note   Half note

Figure 4.4 Simple meter and the beat.

Compound meter
In compound meter, it is more complicated to determine what gets the beat. The bottom number in the time signature **does not** get the beat! In compound meter, three of the bottom number in the time signature gets the beat. Alternately, divide the bottom number by two and add a dot to determine what gets the beat. In ⁶⁄₈, three eighth notes get the beat or one dotted quarter (8 divided by 2 is 4, the quarter note, then add the dot).

Compound Rhythm: What gets the beat?

Dotted half note   Dotted quarter note   Dotted eighth note   Dotted whole note

Figure 4.5 Compound meter and the beat

What gets the beat?

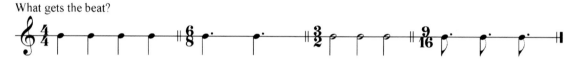

Exercise 4.3 Simple and compound - what gets the beat?

V. How to count in simple and compound rhythms.
Why is counting important? If we are unable to count every note and rest, we won't be able to perform music accurately. That is obvious. However if we are even slightly inaccurate in **writing** music, the problems generated are significant. The professional musician is like a race car driver – they read music down the road at high speeds. If the written music deviates in any way from standard notation and what is expected, the professional musician slams to a stop, crashing against the wall, unable to sight-read.

In counting music you need a number or fraction under every note or rest. Every whole number (1, 2, 3, etc.) needs to be written out. For example if there is a measure with four beats containing two half notes, the numbers '1 2' must be written under the first half note and the numbers '3 4' written under the second note. Rests also must have counts written underneath of them.

counts:1 2   3 4   1   2   3   4

Figure 4.6 Counting simple rhythm

Compound Rhythm

In compound rhythm there are two choices for counting: you can count the beats or the subdivisions of the beat. For example in ⁶⁄₈ you can count to 6 (the subdivisions of the beat). This is a simple way to count but can get confusing if we then think the eighth note gets the beat. This is a source of misunderstanding for students who count the subdivision of the beat and assume it is the beat.

counts: 1   2   3   4   5   6

Figure 4.7 Compound rhythm ⁶⁄₈ with eighth notes and counting to 6.

The other method of counting in compound meter, is to count the beat. In ⁶⁄₈ there are two beats. Remember to divide the top number in the time signature by three to get the number of beats in compound meter. If a measure contains only two dotted quarter notes, the count under the first dotted quarter note would be 1 and the count under the second dotted quarter note would be 2.

counts: 1   2

Figure 4.8 Compound rhythm in ⁶⁄₈: counting the beat

Write in the counts.

Exercise 4.4 Write in the counts in compound rhythm, ⁶⁄₈ dotted quarter and eighth notes.

VI. How to count subdivisions of the beat

Counting subdivisions of the beat in simple meter uses '&' (pronounced 'and') to count the subdivisions of the beat, and 'e & a' for further subdivisions. In ³⁄₄ meter, with a quarter note, two eighth notes and four sixteenth notes, the count would be '1 2 & 3e&a' as shown in Figure 4.9. Notice the counts are lined up exactly under each note.

counts: 1   2   &   3   e   &   a

Figure 4.9 Counting in simple meter: ³⁄₄

VII. Meter classification

Why do we care about meter classification? All meter with the same classification can sound the same. Why do composers choose one meter over another? Cultural and personal bias usually governs choice of meter. Five hundred years ago triple meter was considered perfect and white note rhythms (lots of whole notes, breves, and half notes) the norm, so the pages looked more white, and meters of $\frac{3}{2}$ or $\frac{4}{2}$ were not unusual. Today quadruple meter is the most common and the quarter note most often used. Common meter is another name today for $\frac{4}{4}$ meter. The meters $\frac{4}{2}$ and $\frac{4}{4}$ are both simple quadruple and can sound exactly the same. The only difference is in the ease of reading for today's musician. If a piece is written in $\frac{4}{2}$, amateur performers will not be as familiar with the meter and will find it harder to read. This is not a problem for a professional musician as they will be able to read $\frac{4}{2}$ or $\frac{4}{4}$ with equal ease.

As mentioned in Chapter Two, meter classification has two words. The first word is either simple or compound and identifies the usual subdivision of the beat (simple is in two and compound is in three). The second term is either duple, triple, or quadruple and indicates how many beats are in a measure. Some examples of compound and simple meter classifications are shown in Figure 4.10 and Figure 4.11.

      Compound duple   Compound triple   Compound quadruple

Figure 4.10 Compound meter and meter classification

    Simple quadruple   Simple quadruple   Simple triple   Simple duple

Figure 4.11 Simple meter and meter classification

What is the meter classification?

Exercise 4.5 What is the meter classification?

VIII. Meter is not connected to tempo

Many students believe that meter is connected to tempo and that the meter $\frac{4}{8}$ is faster then $\frac{4}{4}$. This is NOT true. Meter is independent of tempo. Tempo markings are marked separately and chosen by the composer as discussed in Chapter Three. In Figure 4.12 the two measures have different meters but have the same meter classification and will sound exactly the same. In the first measure the quarter note gets the beat and is played at a rate of $\quarternote = 108$. In the second measure the eighth note gets the beat and is played at a rate of $\eighthnote = 108$. Both measures are simple quadruple and the result is the same.

Figure 4.12 Metronome markings in $\frac{4}{8}$ and $\frac{4}{4}$

IX. How many beats?

To determine the number of beats in a given meter, the first question is what gets the beat? In simple meter the answer is the number on the bottom of the time signature. For $\frac{4}{4}$ meter, the quarter note gets the beat. Then we can assign a beat value for every note and rest. If the sixteenth note gets the beat in $\frac{4}{16}$ meter, what fraction of a beat does the thirty-second note get? One half the beat is the correct answer. See Figure 4.13 for a breakdown of how many beats every note would get in $\frac{4}{16}$ meter.

beats: 2 beats   1 beat   1/2 beat   1/2 beat
counts: 1 2   3   4   &

Figure 4.13 Beats for notes and rests in $\frac{4}{16}$ meter

Once you know how many beats every note gets, then you can add up the number of beats for beamed group of notes. Each beamed group usually adds to one beat.

In Figure 4.14, how many beats are in the two measures of $\frac{4}{16}$ meter? The answer is found by first writing the number of beats each note gets (or fraction of a beat), circling the beat groups, writing in the counts, then adding up the total number of counts. The answer is 8 beats.

beats: 1/2   1/2   1   1/2   1/2   1   2   1/2   1/2   1
counts: 1   &   2   3   &   4   12   3   &   4

Figure 4.14 Beats in $\frac{4}{16}$ meter

How many beats?

Exercise 4.6 How many beats does this group of notes in $\frac{4}{16}$ get?

How many beats?

Exercise 4.7 How many beats does this group of notes in $\frac{4}{8}$ meter get?

Homework 6

I. How many beats in each problem. Some measures are not complete. Write in the counts.

Counts _____

Beats _____   _____   _____   _____

Counts _____

Beats _____   _____   _____   _____   _____

II. Rewrite the notes and beam corrrectly in the given meter. Write in the counts.
Some measures might not be complete.

Counts _____

Counts _____

III. Insert barlines. If the final measure is complete, put in the final barline. Write in the counts.

Counts _____

Counts _____

IV. If the measures below are one full measure and are beamed correctly, are they simple or compound?
Write in the counts. What is the meter and meter classification? (simple duple, compound triple, etc.)

Counts _____
Meter _____   _____   _____   _____
meter classification

Counts _____
Meter _____   _____   _____   _____
meter classification

Homework 7

I. How many beats in each problem. Some measures are not complete. Write in the counts.

Counts _____

Beats _____

Counts _____

Beats _____

II. Rewrite the notes and beam corrrectly in the given meter. Write in the counts.
Some measures are not complete

Counts _____

Counts _____

III. Insert barlines. If the final measure is complete, put in the final barline. Write in the counts.

Counts _____

Counts _____

IV. If the measures below are one full measure and are beamed correctly, are they simple or compound?
Write in the counts. What is the meter and meter classification? (simple duple, compound triple, etc.)

Counts _____
Meter _____
meter classification _____

Counts _____
Meter _____
meter classification

Chapter Five: Rhythm and Beaming

I. What gets the beat?

To beam correctly we must understand counting and beats. To begin we ask 'what gets the beat?' In simple meter the bottom number of the time signature gets the beat. For example in $\frac{4}{4}$ the quarter note gets the beat. In $\frac{4}{8}$ meter the eighth note gets one beat.

Simple Rhythm: What gets the beat?

Figure 5.1 Simple meters, what gets the beat?

In compound meter time signature, three of the bottom number gets the beat (or divide the bottom number by two and add a dot)

Compound Rhythm: What gets the beat?

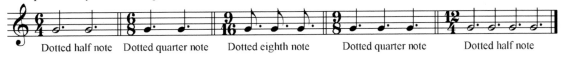

Figure 5.2 Compound meters, what gets the beat?

What gets the beat?

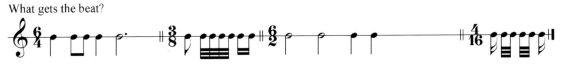

Exercise 5.1 What gets the beat in simple and compound meters?

II. Rules for counting
Simple Meter
In simple meter, the bottom number of the time signature tells what gets the beat and the top number tells the number of beats in a measure. When counting in simple meter, we start at 1 and count to the top number in the time signature. There must be a count for every note or rest. When writing in counts, line up counts directly under the note where the count starts (not centered under notes that are tied). Every whole number (1 2 3 4 etc.) must be written. For fractions of the beat, if there is no note or rest, no count needs to be written.

Figure 5.3 Simple meter - quarter note gets the beat and counts

If eighth note gets the beat, scale down the counts and use the same concepts.

Figure 5.4 Simple meter, eighth note gets the beat and counts

Write in the counts.

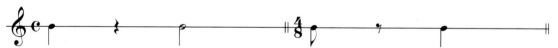

Exercise 5.2 Write in the counts for simple meter, with no subdivisions

Counting subdivisions of the beat
For counting in simple meter use '1 &' for subdivisions of the beat.

Figure 5.5 Simple meter, ⁴⁄₄, counting eighth notes.

For further subdivisions, for sixteenth notes in ⁴⁄₄ times signature use the counts '1 e & a.'

1   2   3   &   4   e   &   a

Figure 5.6 Counting in simple meter: ⁴⁄₄, four 16th notes

If the eighth note gets the count, the same principle applies.

1   2   3   &   4   e   &   a

Figure 5.7 Counting in simple meter: ⁴⁄₈

Write in the counts.

Exercise 5.3 Write in the counts for simple meter with subdivisions

Counting in Compound Meter
There are two counting methods for counting in compound meter. There are advantages to each.
Method 1: In compound meter you can count the beat. In ⁶⁄₈ there are two beats per measure. One measure in ⁶⁄₈ with two dotted quarter notes would be counted 1 2 as shown in Figure 5.8. Each beat, each dotted quarter note, gets one count.

1   2

Figure 5.8 Counting the beat in compound meter

If there is very little rhythmic activity, counting by the beat is very concise and clear and shows the beat by the counting method.

Method 2: When counting in compound meter you can alternatively count the subdivisions of the beat. If in ⁶⁄₈ there are 6 eighth notes, you can count the eighth notes; count to 6; 1 2 3 4 5 6 as shown in Figure 5.9.

Figure 5.9 Counting the subdivisions of the beat in compound meter

The advantage of method 2 is when there are subdivisions of the subdivisions. If in ⁶⁄₈ there are 16th notes, counting is easy when you count the eighth notes. Just add '&' to each number to divide the subdivisions of the beat, the eighth notes, into two sixteenth notes.

Figure 5.10 Compound meter, counting subdivisions in ⁶⁄₈

And if we subdivide even further we can use '1 e & a' just like counting in simple meter.

Figure 5.11 Compound meter, counting subdivisions of the subdivisions in ⁶⁄₈

The disadvantage of this method is that it doesn't show the beat with the counting method so many students get confused and consider the count the beat. And if there is nothing happening in a measure you still have to write all counts. If there is only a dotted half note in a ⁶⁄₈ measure, you still have to count to 6.

Figure 5.12 Compound meter, counting the beat in ⁶⁄₈

This is both good and bad in performance. At slow tempos it is more difficult to maintain a steady beat if only counting to two (the beat in ⁶⁄₈) as in method 1. At very slow tempos, counting to 6 in ⁶⁄₈, will enable the performer to keep a more stable beat.

Method 1 (with subdivisions): In method 1 if there are subdivisions of the beat in a measure, add the syllables 'la' and 'le' to the count. If in a measure of ⁶⁄₈ meter there are 6 eighth notes, the count is '1 la le 2 la le' as shown in Figure 5.13.

Figure 5.13 ⁶⁄₈ measure with 6 eighth notes and counts '1 la le 2 la le.'

With subdivisions of the subdivisions, for example 16th notes in ⁶⁄₈ meter, insert the syllable 'ta': for two eighth notes and two sixteenth notes the count would be '1 la le ta 2 la le ta' as shown in Figure 5.14.

Figure 5.14 Counting subdivisions of the subdivisions of the beat in ⁶⁄₈ with method 1.

There is no counting method for further subdivisions with this method.

Write in the counts.

Exercise 5.4 Compound meters and write in counts

III. General rules for counting
1. When writing counts, just write the numbers or syllables. Don't add commas or parentheses. Write all in one line, with no superscripts, no subscripts, and write clearly.
2. Write a count where the note starts, not centered under tied notes or in the spaces after the note.
3. Write out all whole numbers (1, 2, 3, 4, 5, etc.) up to the number of beats per measure or counts (or subdivisions of the beat as in compound meter). Be consistent. Don't change counting methods in the middle of a measure or piece.

4. Always start over at the number '1' after the bar line at the beginning of each measure.
5. There must be a count written under every note and rest.
6. Start at a whole number (1, 2, 3, 4, etc.) after beamed, beat groups for simple meter and for counting method 2 (counting subdivisions of the beat) for compound meter.

IV. Rules for beaming and writing rhythm
How do we beam? By the beat.

In writing rhythms there are the six general rules to follow.

1. Show the beat.
When beaming or using dots and ties, show the beat.

Figure 5.15 Beaming and writing rhythm to show the beat

2. Be concise.
Where ever possible use the fewest number of notes while still maintaining clarity and showing the beat. Write rhythms with the fewest number of notes possible while still following the other rules.

Figure 5.16 Beaming and writing rhythm to be concise

3. Follow conventions.
Some rhythmic figures that obscure the beat are acceptable because they follow standard conventions. Some syncopated figures have become established norms through common usage in music.

Figure 5.17 Beaming and writing rhythm to follow conventions.

Some rules can be superseded by others. If a rhythm is concise and clear, and follows standard conventions, it might obscure the beat and yet still be acceptable.

4. Be clear.
Sometimes you can obscure a beat and this is acceptable as long as it is clear. In simple quadruple rhythm, you could have a dotted half note followed by a quarter note. This obscures beats 2 and 3 but is very clear, so it is acceptable.

1 2 3   4

Figure 5.18 Writing rhythms that are clear.

5. Notes beamed together or in the same beat and tied together should be combined into one note if possible.

Figure 5.19 Beaming and writing rhythm that is beamed and tied together

6. In quadruple meters, the middle of the measure must be shown. For example, in $\frac{4}{4}$, you can obscure beats 2 and 4 but must show beats 1 and 3.

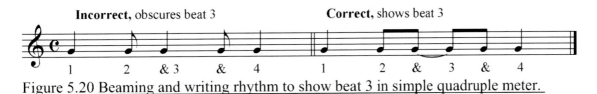

Figure 5.20 Beaming and writing rhythm to show beat 3 in simple quadruple meter.

Fuzzy rule 7. In triple meters you can obscure beat 2 or 3 but not both. It is more common to obscure beat 2 than 3.

Figure 5.21 Beaming and writing rhythm to show beat 2 or 3 in simple triple

Write in the counts.

Exercise 5.5 Is this measure written correctly? If not rewrite it correctly.

V. When can we use dots?
Dotted notes are acceptable unless they obscure the beat or make the rhythm unclear. For quadruple meter you can have a dotted quarter on beat 1 or beat 3 followed by a eighth note, but not on beat two (see Figure 5.19).

Figure 5.22 ¼ Acceptable use of dotted notes showing beat 3

If you wanted a dotted quarter on beat 2, you would need to rewrite it using ties to show beat 3 clearly, as shown in the second measure.

How many beats?

Exercise 5.6 How many beats or fractions of the beat?

Add one note to complete the measure.

Exercise 5.7 Add one note to an incomplete measure to complete it in the given meter.

Insert barlines and write in the counts.

Exercise 5.8 Insert bar lines for given meter

VI. Borrowed subdivisions

The usual subdivisions in simple meter are in groupings of 2 and 4. To subdivide rhythmically into groups of three in simple meter, a special indication is needed. A superscript 3 above three notes with a beam or bracket means play these three notes in the space of two notes. The bracketed group of three notes is called a triplet. In Figure 5.23 a '3' is shown above three eighth notes in $\frac{4}{4}$ meter. This means to play the three notes in the space of two notes. Both notations for the triplet are correct.

Figure 5.23 Triplets in simple meter

The usual subdivisions in compound meter are in groups of three. To indicate a subdivision into groups of 2 or 4 the superscript and brackets are used. If a '2' appears above two beamed eighth notes in $\frac{6}{8}$ meter, it means to play the two notes in the space of three eighth notes. The two notes are called duplets.

Figure 5.24 Duplets in compound meter

When there are triplets in simple meter or duplets in compound meter, these are called borrowed divisions. Borrowed divisions such as triplets and duplets are a good indication of meter type. When we see triplets in the score this indicates that the usual subdivisions are not in 3, so the meter is simple. If duplets are seen in the score, this indicates that the usual subdivision is not in 2 so the meter is compound.

Triplet division with superscript so this is simple meter with four beats per measure - simple quadruple.

Figure 5.25 Identification of simple meter with borrowed subdivisions

Figure 5.26 Identification of compound meter with borrowed subdivisions

If the notes are beamed, the brackets are optional.

Counting Borrowed Subdivisions
We borrow the counting scheme of the meter with the borrowed subdivision. For example if we have triplets in simple meter, as in Figure 5.27, we count them '2 la le.'

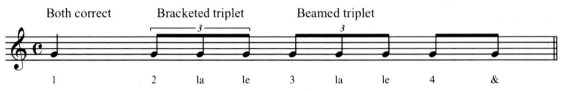

Figure 5.27 Counting triplets

In compound meter we count duplets '1 &, 2 &.'

Figure 5.28 Counting duplets in compound meter.

Homework 8

I. Write in counts. How many beats in each problem

counts _____

_____ beats   _____ beats   _____ beats

II. Identify meter (2/4 3/4, etc.) and meter type (simple duple, compound triple, etc.).
    Write in counts.

counts _____

III. Rewrite below with correct bar lines and beams.
    1.   If the final measure is complete, put in the final bar line. Write in counts.

counts _____

    2.

counts _____

IV. Rewrite to show the meter using correct beaming, dots and ties. Write in counts.
    1.

counts _____

    2.

counts _____

    3.

counts _____

Chapter Six: Major Scales

I. Major Scales: half steps and whole steps

Scales are collections of notes. A common scale is the major scale. As the basis for many songs, the major scale is familiar and happy sounding. In Figure 6.1 is a folk song based on the major scale.

Figure 6.1 A song with a major scale, Row row row your boat

We can start on any note and create a major scale by using the following pattern of whole steps and half steps. Whole step, whole step, half step, whole step, whole step, whole step, half step (WS WS HS WS WS WS HS).

If we start on the note C and follow this pattern, we will play every white key until the next C an octave higher. Remember there is a HS between the notes E and F and between B and C. This is easily demonstrated on the keyboard: there is no black key in between these notes.

C Major scale

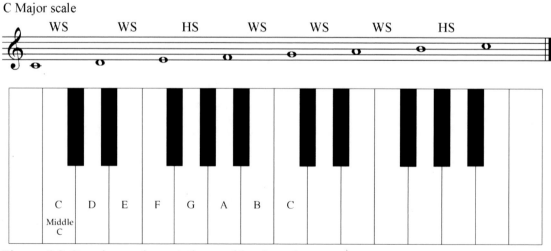

Figure 6.2 C major scale, notation and keyboard

If we start on the note G and follow the same pattern, the result is the G major scale.

G Major scale

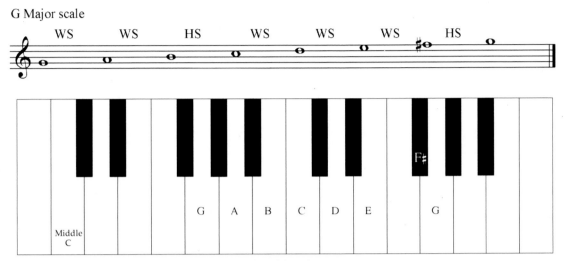

Figure 6.3 G major scale, notation and keyboard

The resultant G major scale has a one sharp, F♯, and no F natural.

If we start on the note D what is the result?

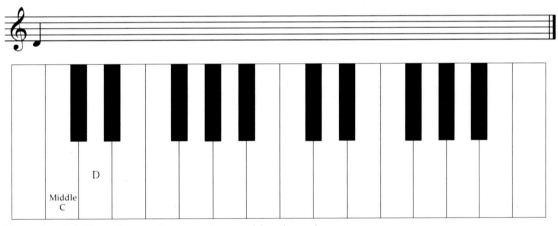

Exercise 6.1 D major scale, notation and keyboard

To notate a scale follow these steps:
1. Write out one of every note, with no duplicates and no skipped notes. Leave space for writing in the accidentals. Start and end on the same note.
2. Count up using the WS WS HS WS WS WS HS pattern to correctly place the accidentals.
3. Put accidentals before the note, on the same line or space as the note they modify.

Safety checks – did you do it right?
1. Did you start and end on the same note with the same accidental or no accidental?
2. Is there a HS between the third and fourth notes, and the seventh and eighth notes?
3. You shouldn't have both sharps and flats in the same major scale – one or the other, but not both.

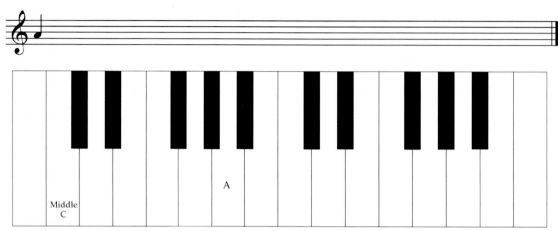

Exercise 6.2 Notate a major scale on A.

You might notice that for the keys C, G, D, A, E, B, F♯, C♯ an additional sharp is added each time.

For the keys of F, B♭, E♭, A♭, D♭, G♭, C♭ an additional flat is added each time. You can now write out all the major scales in Homework 9.

II. Scales and scales degree

Each note of the major scale is called by a scale degree number $\hat{1}$, $\hat{2}$, $\hat{3}$, $\hat{4}$, $\hat{5}$, $\hat{6}$, $\hat{7}$, $\hat{1}$. The little 'hats' on each number indicates that they are scale degrees.

Each scale degree also has a name. Musicians refer to the notes of scale by these names. The most important is the first scale degree, which is called the tonic. The next most important note in any key is the fifth of the scale, and is called the dominant. The rest of the note names are derived from these two names. Immediately above the tonic is the supertonic on the second scale degree. Below the dominant is the fourth scale degree and is called the subdominant. Below the tonic is the seventh scale degree and is called the leading tone because it leads to the tonic. That leaves two scale degree: the third and sixth. Both are called middle notes. The third scale degree is called the mediant (middle) because it is half way between the tonic and dominant. The sixth scale degree is called submediant because it half way between the tonic and subdominant below.

A major scale

tonic   supertonic   mediant   subdominant   dominant   submediant   leading tone   tonic

Figure 6.4 A major scale and scale degrees

Scale Degree	Name
1	Tonic
2	Supertonic
3	Mediant
4	Subdominant
5	Dominant
6	Submediant
7	Leading tone

Figure 6.5 Scale degree names

Once we have all the scales written out we can find out any scale degree of any scale.

What is the tonic of D♭ scale? The tonic is always the same as the name of the scale. What is the dominant of the D♭ scale? Start on D and count up five notes including the first note, the tonic: D, E, F, G, A. So the answer is A something: A♮, A♭, or A♯. To find the answer look at the D♭ scale and look at the fifth scale degree, which is A♭.

D♭ major scale

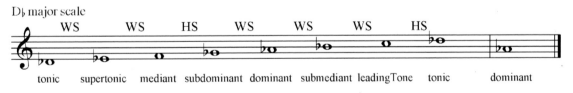

tonic   supertonic   mediant   subdominant   dominant   submediant   leadingTone   tonic   dominant

Figure 6.6 D♭ scale and what is the dominant?

What is the tonic of E♭? What is the subdominant of E♭?

Exercise 6.3 Scale degree and scales. What is the tonic of E♭? The subdominant of E♭?

III. Writing descending scales

Descending scales are created the same way as ascending scales but the pattern goes
backwards. To notate a descending F major scale, start on F and write out the descending
scale with one of everything, no repeats and no skips, all white notes (no accidentals),
until you get to F an octave lower. To figure out the correct accidentals, either start at the
top and do the major scale whole step – half step pattern backwards (HS WS WS WS HS
WS WS). Or, start with the bottom note and do the original pattern (WS WS HS WS WS
WS HS), just move along the notes backwards, that is move right to left.

F major scale

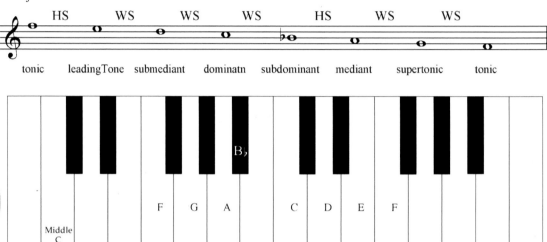

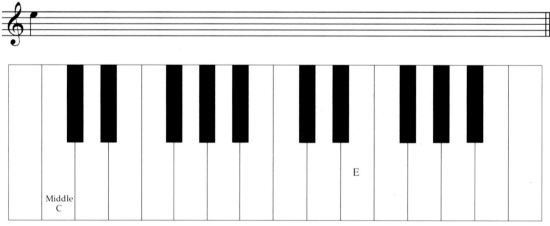

Figure 6.7 Descending F major scale with WS and HS

Notate a descending E major scale.

Exercise 6.4 Write out a descending E major scale

Homework 9

I. Write out ascending major scales on each starting pitch in both clefs. Add accidentals as needed to create the major scale pattern, WS WS HS WS WS WS HS. Bracket HS.

F, 1b

Ab 4b

Bb 2b

C # D

Eb 3b

II. Write out the ascending major scale on each starting pitch in the given clef.

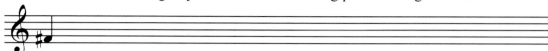

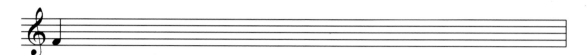

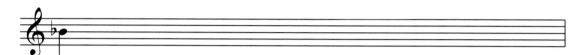

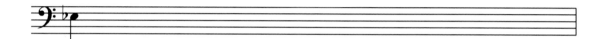

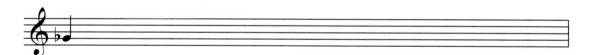

Homework 10

I. Identify and notate the requested notes. The first problem is done.

1. Dominant in G   2. Subdominant in F 3. Supertonic in D♭   4. Leading tone in F♯ 5. Tonic in D♭

_____D

6. Submediant in E♭   7. Subdominant in A♭ 8. Mediant in E   9. Leading tone in F 10. Subdominant in B

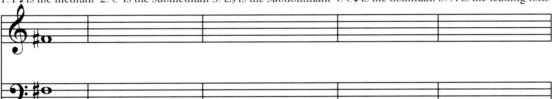

11. Supertonic in D   12. Dominant in B♭ 13. Leading tone in G♭ 14. Subdominant in A 15. Dominant in C♭

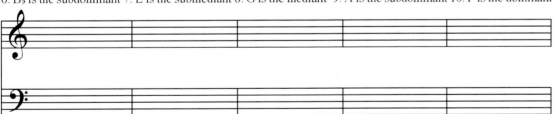

II. Identify the key (the tonic) and notate the note in both staves.

1. F♯ is the mediant 2. C is the submediant 3. E♭ is the subdominant 4. C♯ is the dominant 5. A is the leading tone

Key: _D Major_____

6. B♭ is the subdominant 7. E is the submediant 8. G is the mediant 9. A is the subdominant 10. F is the dominant

Key:_____

11. A♭ is the subdom. 12. D♭ is the dominant 13. B is the mediant 14. C is the supertonic 15. F is the submediant

Key:_____

III. Write out the descending major scale on the following notes using the same major scale pattern. Remember to use the pattern backwards. Locate and bracket HS.

Chapter Seven: Major Key Signatures

I. What is a key signature?

A key signature is found at the beginning of a line of music and shows which notes will always use accidentals. This saves time and space in writing music, as the accidental can be written out once on each line instead of every time we play the note. In keys with many sharps or flats such as the key of C♯ major or C♭ minor, this makes the music much cleaner and easier to read.

C♯ major scale with accidentals   C♯ major scale with key signature

Figure 7.1 C♯ major with accidentals and a key signature

II. Major Scales: using key signatures.

If you select any note and know the set of sharps or flats to use, you don't have to count WS and HS to figure out the scale. Each major scale uses a different set of either sharps or flats, not both. This set of sharps or flats is called the key signature for each scale. Below is a table that lists all the major key signatures. Each key signature starts with the same sharp (F♯) or flat (B♭) and adds one more sharp or flat for the next key signature.

Major Key	# sharps/flats	What are #/♭
C	0	
G	1 ♯	F♯
D	2 ♯	F♯ C♯
A	3 ♯	F♯ C♯ G♯
E	4 ♯	F♯ C♯ G♯ D♯
B	5 ♯	F♯ C♯ G♯ D♯ A♯
F♯	6 ♯	F♯ C♯ G♯ D♯ A♯ E♯
C♯	7 ♯	F♯ C♯ G♯ D♯ A♯ E♯ B♯
F	1 ♭	B♭
B♭	2 ♭	B♭ E♭
E♭	3 ♭	B♭ E♭ A♭
A♭	4 ♭	B♭ E♭ A♭ D♭
D♭	5 ♭	B♭ E♭ A♭ D♭ G♭
G♭	6 ♭	B♭ E♭ A♭ D♭ G♭ C♭
C♭	7 ♭	B♭ E♭ A♭ D♭ G♭ C♭ F♭

We can memorize all the key signatures for every key, but there is an easier way to learn key signatures using the Circle of Fifths.

III. Circle of Fifths

How do we get to know the key signatures for all the major scales? A useful tool for learning all the key signatures for major scales is to know the Circle of Fifths. Like a clock it tells how many sharps or flats are in each key.

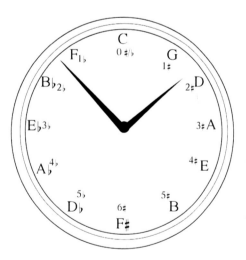

Figure 7.2a Circle fifths for major keys

How do we remember them? A mnemonic device is helpful. Have a sentence that starts with the first letter of each key name. Fast Cars Go Down Alleys Every Block or F C G D A E B.

We start one tick to the left of 12 o'clock on the circle and write in F, then write in each of the corresponding letters on each station of the clock. At 5 o'clock we have run out of letters, so we start over using sharps, F♯, C♯. At 7 o'clock we stop because we don't go past 7 sharps in a key since a key with 7 sharps has a sharp on every note.

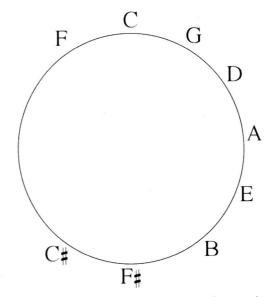

Figure 7.2b Circle fifths for major keys: sharp keys

Then we add the keys that have flats in the key signature. We can use another sentence for flats: Better Eat Another Dozen Good Chickens or B E A D G C. We start to the left of F at 10 o'clock and move counterclockwise. Every flat key has a flat in the name except for F. B♭, E♭, A♭, D♭ (D♭ is enharmonic to C♯ so write a slash by C♯ and D♭ next to it), G♭ (enharmonic to F♯), and C♭ (enharmonic to B). Don't go past C♭ which has 7 flats and all notes are flat.

The Circle of Fifths shows all the major key signatures and the number of sharps or flats in each. You can label each with the number of sharps or flats or just know that the circle is like a clock. At 3 o'clock is A. It has three sharps. At 9 o'clock the key is E♭ and it mirrors A with 3 flats. There are three sets of enharmonic keys. At 6 o'clock are F♯ and G♭ with six accidentals each. C♯/D♭ have 7♯ and 5♭ and C♭/B have 7♭ and 5♯ respectively. Notice the key of C major has no sharps or flats, while the keys of C♯ and C♭ have all sharps and flats.

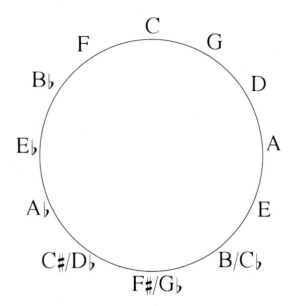

Figure 7.2c Circle fifths for major keys

Exercise 7.1 Draw the Circle of fifths with all major keys within 3 minutes

IV. Order of sharps and flats

The same sentence that we use for learning the Circle of Fifths can be used for learning the order of sharps: Fast Cars Go Down Alleys Every Block. F♯ C♯ G♯ D♯ A♯ E♯ B♯
The same sentence backwards gives the order of flats. Or we can use the second sentence: Better Eat Another Dozen Good Chicken Fingers. B♭ E♭ A♭ D♭ G♭ C♭ F♭

Each time we add a sharp or flat to the key signature, we keep the previous sharps and flats and add one more. The key of G has one sharp, F♯, the key of D has two sharps, F♯ and C♯, and the key of A has three sharps, F♯, C♯, and G♯.

Exercise 7.2 Write out the order of sharps and flats

V. How to write sharps and flats for key signatures

When writing key signatures, sharps and flats are written in specific places on each clef with no variations. If you begin with the sharps on F line and C space for the treble clef, each subsequent sharp is written a step up, aligned in its own vertical space. The A♯ is written an octave lower so the sharp isn't written with a ledger line in the treble clef. The bass clef follows the same pattern, mirroring the treble clef.

For flat keys, start with flats on the lines for B♭ and E♭. Add each additional flat a step
below the B♭ and the E♭ respectively. All flats flow downwards.

Figure 7.3 Key signatures for sharp keys

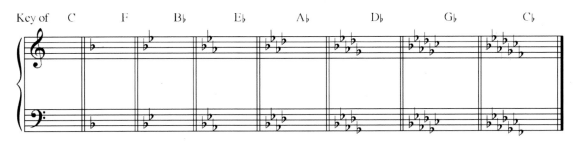

Figure 7.4 Key signatures for flat keys

Exercise 7.3 Write the key signature for E♭? For F♯? For D♭

VI. How to write out scales with or without key signatures.
If we use a key signature to write out a scale, we first write the key signature for that
scale. Then we start on tonic note and write out the scale, with no skips and no
duplications, starting and ending on the same note. That's it.

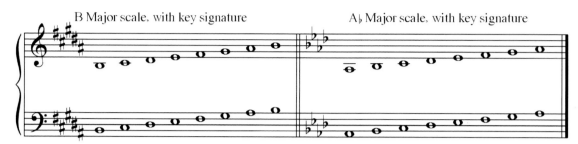

Figure 7.5 B major and A♭ major scale with key signatures

If we want to write out the scale without a key signature, our task is a little harder. We write out the scale starting on the tonic with no skips and no duplications, starting and ending on the same note, and leaving space for writing in the accidentals. Then we look at the key signature for that key and write in all of the accidentals.

Figure 7.6 B major scale and A♭ major scale with accidentals

Exercise 7.4 Notate the F♯ scale using accidentals

VII. How to figure out scale degree with key signatures

We can figure out the scale degree of any scale using key signatures. If we want to know the mediant note (third scale degree) of the A major scale, we count up three notes including the first: A, B, C. So C-something is the mediant. Is it C♮, C♭, or C♯? To answer this we look on the Circle of Fifths to determine the key signature for A major. A major is at 3 o'clock on the Circle of Fifths and has three sharps. We know the three sharps are F♯, C♯ and G♯ from the order of sharps.

In the key of A major, C is always C♯ because there are no duplications; you can't have
C♮ and C♯ in the same major scale. So the mediant of A is C♯.

A major scale

mediant

Figure 7.7 The mediant of A major is C♯

Exercise 7.5 Using the Circle of Fifths, what is the dominant of B♭?

VIII. How to get to know the Circle of Fifths?
The Circle of Fifths has a lot of information in it. It gives information about keys, scales,
scale degrees, intervals, chords and chord progressions. It is to your great benefit to know
the Circle of Fifths very well. Drill the Circle of Fifths until you can write all the keys
within one minute. This helps you to know it without figuring it out or thinking about it.

Exercise 7.6 Write the Circle of Fifths in under 2 minutes, then in under 1 minute

Homework 11

I. Write out all major key signatures in both clefs.

II. Draw the Circle of fifths, major keys only.

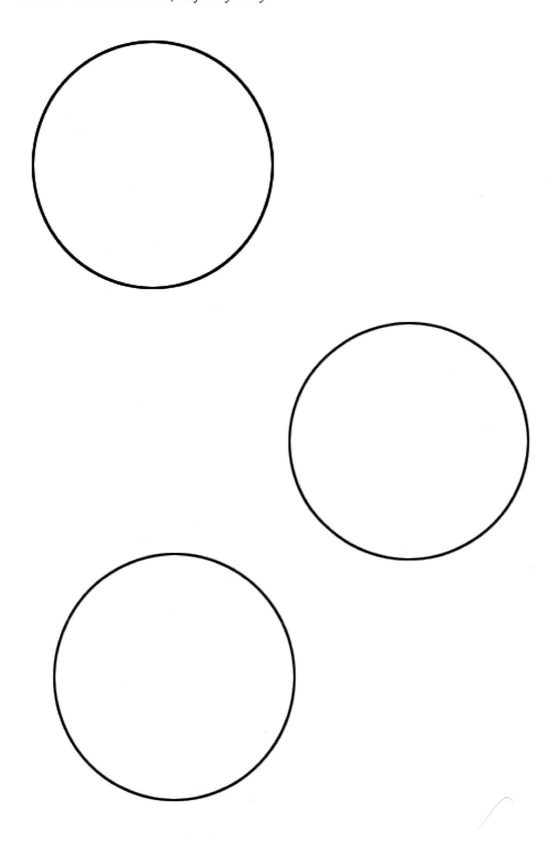

Homework 12 – Midterm Review

I. Identify and locate the notes on the keyboard. Include pitch octave, e.g. D4, C3, etc.

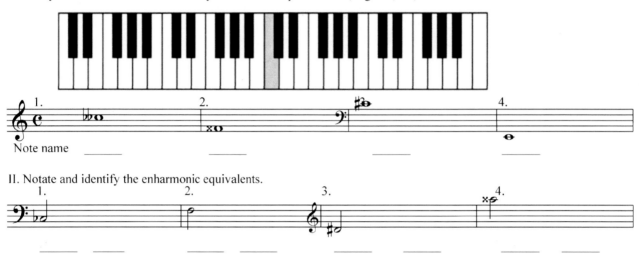

Note name _____   _____   _____   _____

II. Notate and identify the enharmonic equivalents.

_____   _____   _____   _____

III. Identify the pitch including the pitch octave number, then rewrite the given pitch in the other clef.

IV. Rewrite the notes in the clef below using the octava sign

V. How many beats in each problem. Some measures are not complete. Write in the counts.

Counts _____

Counts _____

VI. Insert barlines. If the final measure is complete, put in the final barline. Write in the counts.

Counts _____

VII. Rewrite the notes and beam corrrectly in the given meter. Write in the counts.

Counts _____

Counts _____

VIII. What is the top number in the time signature if this is one measure? Write in the counts.

IX. Notate the scales below in both clefs.

1. A major, ascending, accidentals   2. D♭ major, key signature, ascending

X. Identify and notate the requested notes in both clefs.

1. Dominant in F♯   2. Subdominant in E♭   3. Supertonic in B   4. Leading tone in G♭   5. Mediant in D♭

XI. Identify the key, write the key signature and notate the note.

1. Bb is the dominant   2. F♯ is the submediant   3. Fb is the subdominant   4. Db is the supertonic   5. B♯ is the leading tone

Key: _____

XII. Rewrite notes in the next measure without ties

XIII. Group the notes using beams so that the meter is shown

XIV. Assuming each to be a complete measure with correct beaming, write the correct time signature in each measure

XII. Musical terms

1. What is *pianissimo*?_____

2. What does this mean? *D. C. al fine*_____

3. Draw the repeat sign._____

4. How fast is *Allegro*?_____

5. What does *Largo* mean?_____

6. What happens during a *ritardando*?_____

7. What is a *crescendo*?_____

8. What is the difference between tempo, beat, and meter?_____

_____

Chapter Eight: Minor Key Signatures

w H w w H w w

I. What are minor keys?

A minor key uses the same set of notes as a major key but centers around a different note. The pattern of whole steps and half steps is different, but more importantly the sound is different. In general, minor keys have a recognizably sad sound. This doesn't mean that all sad songs are in a minor key or that every song in a minor key is sad. The A minor scale is shown in Figure 8.1. It uses only the white keys which are the same notes as the C major scale.

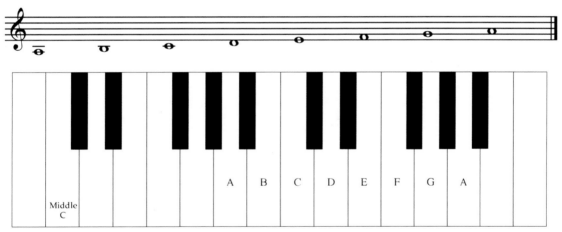

Figure 8.1 A minor scale, keyboard and notation

II. Relative minor keys.

Every minor scale is related to one major scale that is three half steps above the tonic note of the minor key. The two scales share the same key signature and the same set of notes. The minor key that is three HS below a major key is called the relative minor. A minor is the relative minor of C major. Or conversely C major is the relative major of A minor. C major uses all the white keys and centers on the note C. A minor also uses all the white notes but focuses on the note A. The key focus is called the tonal center and is often the note that begins and ends a piece of music. Here are the key signatures for the major keys and their relative minors. Notice the minor keys are denoted by lower case letters while the major keys are denoted by upper case letters.

Major Key	Relative Minor Key	# sharps/flats	What are #/♭
C	a	0	
G	e	1 ♯	F♯
D	b	2 ♯	F♯ C♯
A	f♯	3 ♯	F♯ C♯ G♯
E	c♯	4 ♯	F♯ C♯ G♯ D♯
B	g♯	5 ♯	F♯ C♯ G♯ D♯ A♯
F♯	d♯	6 ♯	F♯ C♯ G♯ D♯ A♯ E♯
C♯	a♯	7 ♯	F♯ C♯ G♯ D♯ A♯ E♯ B♯
F	d	1 ♭	B♭
B♭	g	2 ♭	B♭ E♭
E♭	c	3 ♭	B♭ E♭ A♭
A♭	f	4 ♭	B♭ E♭ A♭ D♭
D♭	b♭	5 ♭	B♭ E♭ A♭ D♭ G♭
G♭	e♭	6 ♭	B♭ E♭ A♭ D♭ G♭ C♭
C♭	a♭	7 ♭	B♭ E♭ A♭ D♭ G♭ C♭ F♭

The key signatures for the minor keys look exactly the same as the major keys. You can't tell if a key is major or minor by looking at the key signature. We can determine if a key is major or minor by listening to it, looking at the starting and ending and predominant notes and chords.

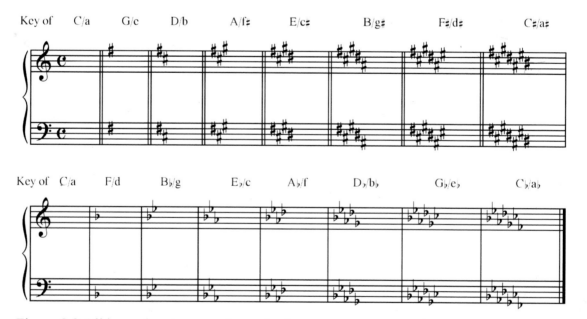

Figure 8.2 All keys signatures, major and minor

Exercise 8.1 Write out the key signature for b♭ minor

III. Circle of Fifths
Information about major and minor key signatures can be learned through knowing the
Circle of Fifths with the major keys on the outside and the relative minor keys on the
inside of the circle. First we write the major keys on the Circle of Fifths using the
mnemonic sentence for the order of sharps and flats and major key signatures: Fast Cars
Go Down Alleys Every Block or F C G D A E B.

Starting one tick to the left of 12 o'clock on the circle, write in F then move clockwise
and write in each of the corresponding letters on each station of the clock. At 5 o'clock
we have run out of letter so we start over using sharps, F♯, C♯. At 7 o'clock we stop
because we don't go past 7 sharps in a key, which has a sharp on every note.

Then we add the flat keys. We use another sentence for flats Better Eat Another Dozen
Good Chicken Fingers or B E A D G C F. We start to the left of F at 10 o'clock and begin
with B♭. Every flat key has a flat in the name, except for F. Moving counter clockwise we
write the flat keys on the Circle of Fifths: B♭, E♭, A♭, D♭ (enharmonic to C♯ so write a slash
by C♯ and D♭ next to it), G♭ (enharmonic to F♯), and C♭ (enharmonic to B). Don't go past
C♭ which 7 flats and all notes are flat.

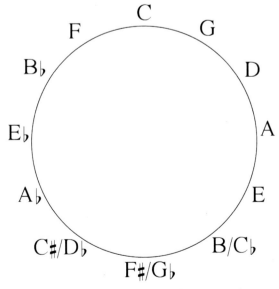

Figure 8.3 Circle of fifth with major keys only

To add the minor keys use the same procedure but start a quarter turn to the left on the inside of the circle. F minor is inside the circle opposite A♭ major. Use our sentence Fast Cars Go Down Alleys Every Block or F C G D A E B to add in the minor keys through 2 sharps. Then begin the sentence again at F but add sharps to the letter names. At three sharps, inside the circle opposite the key of A major is the key of f# minor. Continue clockwise around the circle until you reach 7 sharps with a♯ minor.

To finish the flat keys, start inside the circle opposite D♭ major with 5 flats. Remember the sentence for flats: Better Eat Another Dozen Good Chicken Fingers or B E A D G C F

Most flat keys have a flat in the key name. Add in b♭ minor opposite D♭ major (enharmonic to a# minor so add the slash after a♯ minor and write in b♭ minor). Then write in e♭ minor enharmonic to d♯ minor and then a♭ minor enharmonic to g♯ minor.

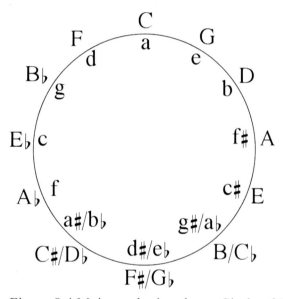

Figure 8.4 Major and minor keys, Circle of Fifths

These are the thirty major and minor keys. Drill writing out the Circle of Fifths, major and minor until you can do this under a minute. At this speed, you will be able to write your Circle of Fifths without having to figure out the key signatures. No need to write out the number of sharps and flats as this information can easily be seen from the placement on the circle. At 3 o'clock is A major and f♯ minor and they both have three sharps in the key signature.

Exercise 8.2 Draw the Circle of fifths, major and minor keys, in 1 minute

Mnemonic sentences are a good way to start to learn the key signatures. But it is only a start. Once you can write the Circle of Fifths quickly using the mnemonic sentences try other approaches. Here are some other ways to write the Circle of Fifths. Try the following five approaches to writing the Circle of Fifths. Do the suggested order first and then fill in the rest of the keys. 1. Write the six enharmonic keys first, major and minor. 2. Write in C/a, C♯/a♯, C♭/a♭ (no ♯/♭ and all ♯/♭). 3. Write in six ♯ and six ♭ (F♯ and G♭). 4. Do the quadrants; zero ♯/♭, 3 ♯/♭, 6 ♯/♭ first (C/a, A/f♯, E♭/c♯, F♯/d♯ and G♭/e♭). 5. Finally, do random access: 1♯, 3♭, 7♯, 4♭, etc. When we get to this last stage, we know the key signatures and we can use this information in musical practice such as composition, jazz improvisation, and analysis.

IV. Key signatures for minor keys
Minor key signatures are written in a same way as major keys; use the order of sharps or flats, with no variations. Key signatures are identical for major and relative minor scales.

Exercise 8.3 Write out the key signature for d♯ minor

When you look at a piece of music how do you know if it is major or minor? First look at the key signature. There are two choices, major and relative minor. To choose between the two, look at the notes that begin or end the piece. Look through the piece and ask, which note is more prevalent, the tonic of the major or relative minor? Also look for tonic and dominant notes in major and minor keys. In a piece with one sharp that begins and ends on the note E and has many E and B notes in it, we would conclude the piece is in e minor. Playing the piece will usually give us the same information. Our ears are often more advanced than our understanding of theory. If the piece sounds happy it is probably major and if it sound more somber, it is likely to be minor.

In Figure 8.5 the key signature has 4 sharps, indicating the key is either E major or C♯ minor. The first three measures begin and end on E, there are three Es, and one B. So we would conclude it is in the key of E major. The last three measures begin and end on C♯, there are three C♯s, and one G. So we conclude the last three measures are in C♯ minor. In the C♯ measures there is also a raised seventh scale degree of the C♯ harmonic minor scale, B♯, which will be discussed in Chapter 9.

Figure 8.5 Phrase in E major, phrase in c♯ minor

What is the key?

Exercise 8.4 What is the key, major or minor?

Homework 13

I. Write out the specified major or minor key signatures in both clefs.

II. Draw the Circle of fifths, major and minor keys.

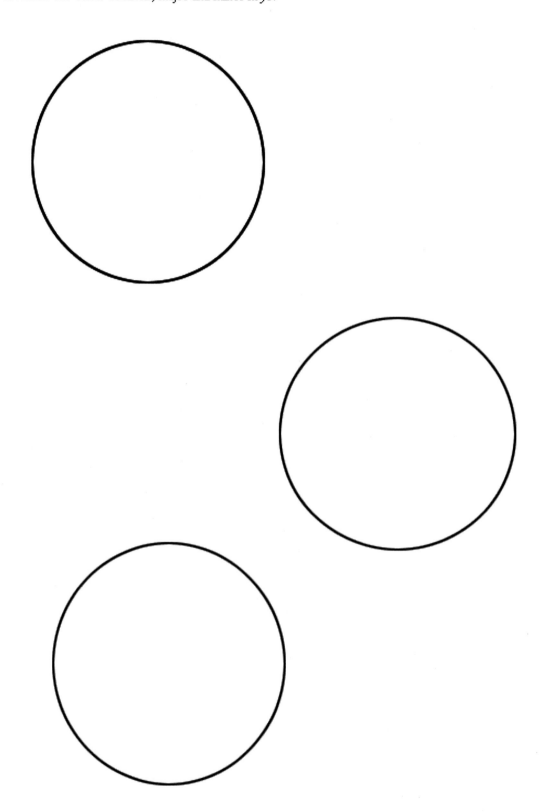

Chapter Nine: Minor Scales

I. Minor scales

Minor scales begin on the tonic of the minor key. We can use a half step and whole step pattern to write minor scales (WS HS WS WS HS WS WS). However it is much faster to use the Circle of Fifths and key signatures to write out minor scales.

The key of A minor has no sharps and flats. To write out the A minor scale in both clefs we begin on the note A and write out the scale with one of each note, no skips, and no repeats. And in this case there are no accidentals, so we are done. This is the A minor scale.

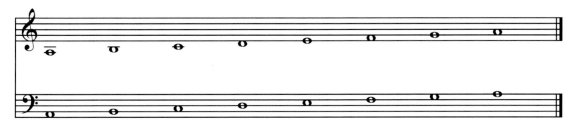

Figure 9.1 A minor scale, both clefs

The key of e minor has one sharp in the key signature. To notate the e minor scale, first write the key signature then write out the scale from e to e, an octave higher. Try this in Exercise 9.1.

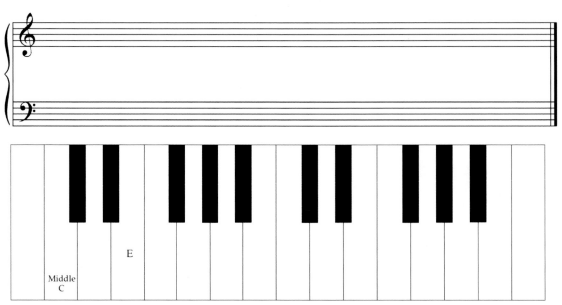

Exercise 9.1 Notate the e minor scale

II. Three types of minor scales
There are three types of minor scales in common use: natural minor, harmonic minor, melodic minor.

Natural minor scale
The natural minor scale contains the same set of notes as the key signature. The scale on A with no sharps or flats is the A minor scale and more specifically, the A natural minor scale. If we know the Circle of Fifths, we know all key signatures, and we know all the natural minor scales. To write out the scale, simply write out the key signature, then beginning on the tonic note, write out the notes of the scale.

In Figure 9.2 the G natural minor scale is notated and shown on the keyboard. First we write the key signature, which has two flats (B♭ and E♭). Then we write the scale from G to G an octave higher and we are done.

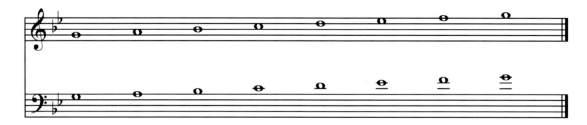

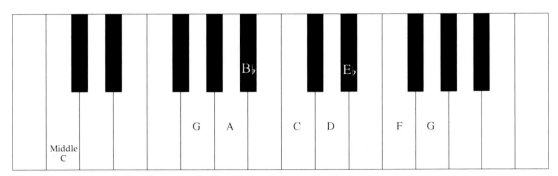

Figure 9.2 G natural minor scale, keyboard and notation.

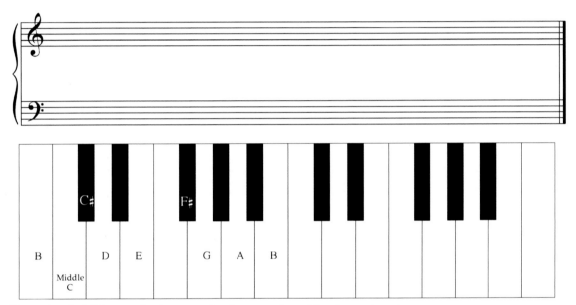

Exercise 9.2 Notate the b natural minor scale with a key signature.

Harmonic minor scale

The harmonic minor scale arose in response to changes in harmony: hence the name harmonic minor. People around 400 years ago began liking a harmony in the minor scale that altered one note. We'll discuss harmony in a later chapter. The change in harmony led to a change in the scale; the seventh scale degree was raised, creating a $\sharp\hat{7}$ in the scale. The natural minor scale with a raised seventh scale degree ($\sharp\hat{7}$), is called the harmonic minor scale. In Figure 9.3 we see the A natural minor scale with the altered seventh scale degree ($\sharp\hat{7}$), which creates the harmonic minor scale.

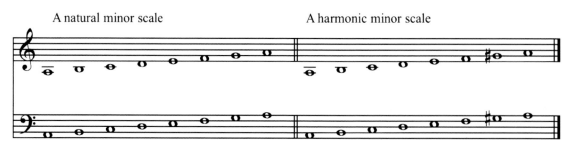

Figure 9.3 A natural and harmonic minor

Any natural minor scale can then be altered by raising the $\hat{7}$ one half step, thereby adding a $\sharp\hat{7}$ to the scale. The raising of the seventh scale degree is always relative to the key signature. If the seventh scale degree had no accidental such as in the key of g minor, it becomes sharp. The seventh scale degree of the g natural minor scale is F. So in the g harmonic minor scale, the raised seventh scale degree, the $\sharp\hat{7}$, is F♯.

If the note was flat in the key signature it becomes natural. In c minor, the $\hat{7}$ is B♭. In c harmonic minor, the $\sharp\hat{7}$ is B♮. If the note was already sharp in the key signature, than it must be raised one more half step and made into a double sharp. In d♯ minor the $\hat{7}$ is C♯. In d♯ harmonic minor the $\sharp\hat{7}$ is C𝄪.

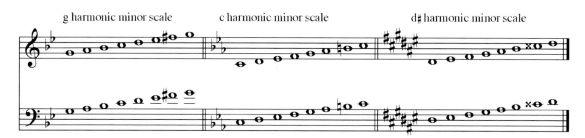

Figure 9.4 Three harmonic minor scales, $\sharp\hat{7}$ in g minor, c minor, d♯ minor

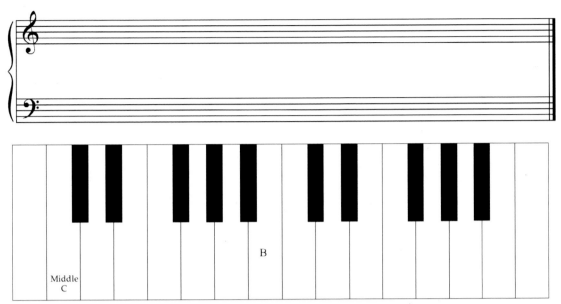

Exercise 9.3 Notate the b harmonic minor scales using a key signature and adding accidentals

Melodic minor scale

When the 7th scale degree was altered in the harmonic minor scale, an interval between the 6th and 7th scale degree was created that was difficult to sing. The sound of this interval (WS + HS), and the resultant scale, was not an accepted or familiar sound in European music at the time.

E harmonic minor scale

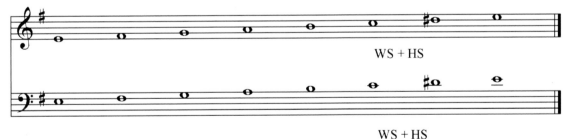

WS + HS

Figure 9.5 Harmonic minor scale, with a WS + HS between $\hat{6}$ and $\sharp\hat{7}$

Composers then began to also raise the 6th scale degree to make the interval between the 6th and 7th scales degrees a WS. The scale that raised the $\hat{6}$ and $\hat{7}$ was called the melodic minor scale because the alterations had to do with melody. The raised 6th and 7th scale degrees smoothly led up to the tonic. On the descending melodic minor scale, the $\hat{6}$ and $\hat{7}$ are returned to the notes of the natural minor scale.

E melodic minor scale

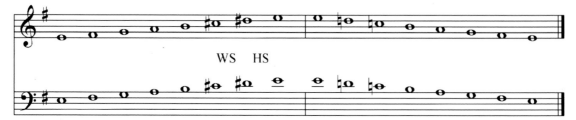

WS   HS

Figure 9.6 Melodic minor scale

The melodic minor scale is the only scale that has different notes when ascending and descending, so the ascending and descending forms must both be written.

Exercise 9.4 Notate the b♭ melodic minor scale using accidentals

III. Why three minor scales?
Natural minor scales came first historically. Music from 1000 years ago used natural minor scales. About 400 years ago tuning systems, aesthetics, and harmonies shifted and the harmonic minor scale was the result. Composers at the time felt that the half step between the leading tone and the tonic gave an appealing propulsion to the music, leading more strongly to the tonic. The resultant scale had an interval between the 6th and 7th scale degrees that was not a culturally accepted sound at the time and was difficult to sing. So the 6th scale degree was raised creating the melodic minor scale.

In practice, all three forms of the minor scale are sometimes used in the same music. Western classical and popular music both use the harmonic and melodic minor scales more often than the natural minor scale. Music that uses the natural minor scale sounds ancient. Folk music from Scotland and England often use natural minor scales.

Why did the scales change?
Music evolves as composers experiment and try new sounds. When the sounds are successful, people like the music. It is played more often and imitated by other composers. More composers then try out the new sounds until they become an accepted and established part of the musical culture. Composers continue to try out new sounds and music continues to evolve. A musical culture is never static but is the culmination of the tastes and preferences of the people who create and listen to the music. There isn't

always a logical reason for a particular scale or style of music to develop. The music of a particular culture is the way people in that culture like music to be played and in this way traditions develop and continue. A musical culture is always specific to a time and place.

In most of today's music, major and minor scales are common. There are thousands of scales in use around the world in different cultures. Each has distinctive sounds, intervals and tunings. Some contemporary classical composers invent new scales for each piece of music that they compose.

IV. Minor scales and scale degree

Each note of the minor scale is called by a scale degree number ($\hat{1}, \hat{2}, \hat{3}, \hat{4}, \hat{5}, \hat{6}, \hat{7}, \hat{1}$) and also a scale degree name. With one exception, the scale degree names are the same as the major scale. The first scale degree is called the tonic and the fifth of the scale is called the dominant. The rest of the note names are derived from these two names. Immediately above the tonic is the supertonic on the second scale degree. Below the dominant is the fourth scale degree and is called the subdominant. The third scale degree is called mediant (middle) because it is half way between the tonic and dominant. The sixth scale degree is called submediant because it half way between the tonic and subdominant below.

In the natural minor scale the seventh scale degree is a whole step below the tonic and is called the subtonic. When it is raised, as in the harmonic minor scale and the melodic minor scale, it is called the leading tone because it leads to the tonic – the same as in the major keys.

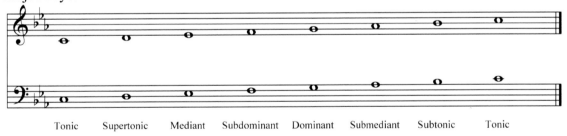

Tonic   Supertonic   Mediant   Subdominant   Dominant   Submediant   Subtonic   Tonic

Scale Degree	Name
$\hat{1}$	Tonic
$\hat{2}$	Supertonic
$\hat{3}$	Mediant
$\hat{4}$	Subdominant
$\hat{5}$	Dominant
$\hat{6}$	Submediant
$\hat{7}$ (natural minor)	Subtonic
$\sharp\hat{7}$	Leading tone

Figure 9.7 C minor scale and scale degrees

If we know the key signatures for all major and minor scales using the Circle of Fifths, we can then calculate any scale degree of any scale.

What is the tonic of b♭ scale? The tonic is always the same as the name of the scale.

What is the dominant of the b♭ scale? Start on b and count up five notes including the first note, the tonic: B, C, D, E, F. The correct answer is F something: F♮, F♭, or F♯. To find the answer look at the key signature for b♭ minor. b♭ has 5 flats in the key signature, B♭, E♭, A♭, D♭, G♭. F is not flat in the key of b♭ minor, so the dominant of b♭ minor is F.

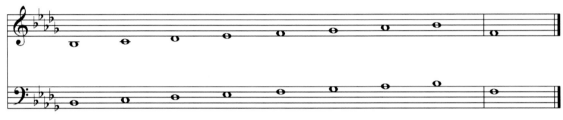

Tonic   Supertonic   Mediant   Subdominant   Dominant   Submediant   Subtonic   Tonic   Dominant

Figure 9.8 What is the dominant of the b♭ scale?

To find the leading tone of b♭ harmonic minor, we go one step below B, which is A. The answer is A something: A♮, A♭, or A♯. We look at the key signature for b♭ minor which has 5 flats in the key signature, B♭, E♭, A♭, D♭, G♭, and see that A is A♭ in the key of b♭ minor. A♭ is the subtonic in b♭ minor. To find the leading tone, we raise the 7th scale degree. If we raise A♭ a half step, we get A♮. So the leading tone of b♭ minor, the #$\hat{7}$, is A♮.

b♭ harmonic minor scale

Tonic   Supertonic   Mediant   Subdominant   Dominant   Submediant   Leading Tone   Tonic   Leading Tone

Figure 9.9 Leading tone in b♭ minor

Exercise 9.5 What is the submediant of g♯?

V. Writing minor scales without key signatures
When writing minor scales without key signatures use the following procedure:
1. Write one of every note, with no duplicates and no skipped notes. Leave space for writing in the accidentals.

2. Determine the key signature for the natural minor scale using the Circle of Fifths.
3. Put the accidentals from the key signature on the same line or space as the note they modify, before the note.
4. For the harmonic minor scale, find the 7th scale degree just below the tonic, and raise it one half step. If it was natural, add a ♯, if it was flat, erase the flat. If it was ♯, make it a double sharp.
5. For the melodic minor scale, find the 6th and 7th scale degrees and raise them each one half step.
6. For the melodic minor, also add the descending form of the scale. Return the 6th and 7th scale degrees to the natural minor scale for the descending scale.

Safety checks: did you do it right?
1. Did you start and end on the same note with the same accidental or no accidental?
2. You shouldn't have both sharps and flats in the same natural minor scale: one or the other but not both (although there could be both sharps and flats in the harmonic and melodic minor scales).
3. In the harmonic and melodic minor scales, check that the 6th and 7th scale degrees are raised in relation to the natural minor key signature. In the harmonic and melodic minor scales there might be sharps and flats in the same key (key of d minor), or sharps and double sharps in the same key (key of a# minor).

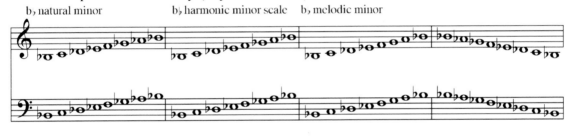

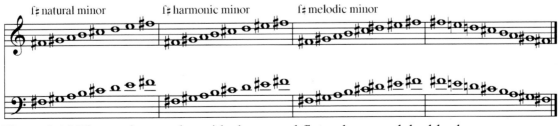

Figure 9.10 Three minor scales with sharps and flats, sharps and double sharps

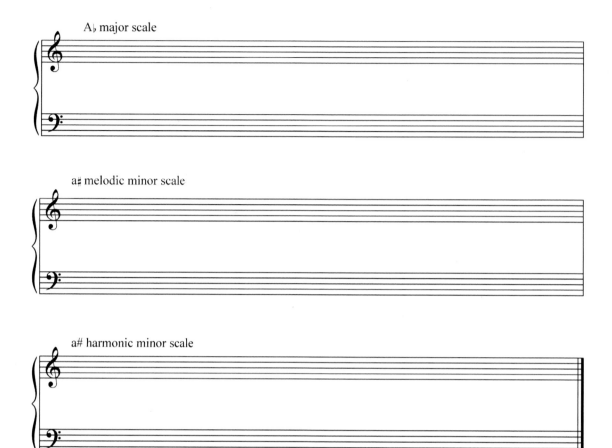

Exercise 9.6 Notate the A♭ major scale, the a♯ melodic minor scale and the a♯ harmonic minor scale

Homework 14

I. Write the ascending natural minor scale using key signatures.

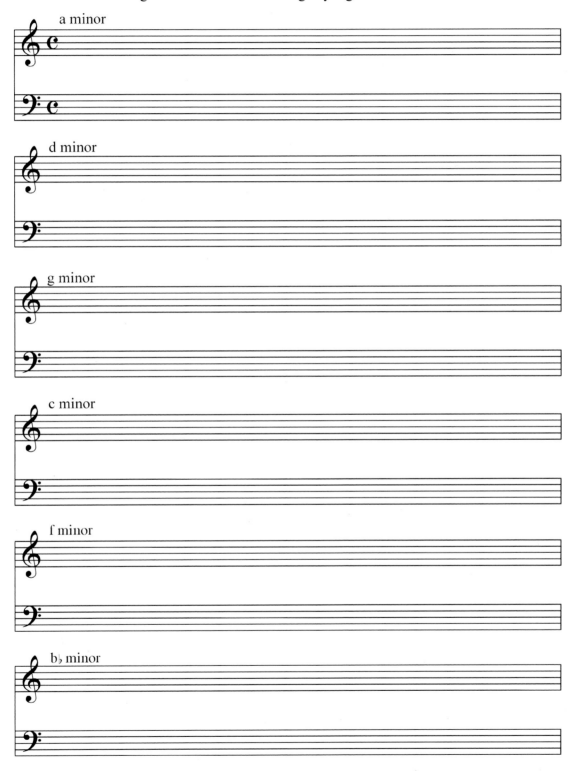

II. Write out the ascending natural minor scale using accidentals.

e♭ minor

a♭ minor

e minor

b minor

f♯ minor

c♯ minor

g♯ minor

d♯ minor

a♯ minor

III. Write out the harmonic minor scales using key signatures

a harmonic minor   e harmonic minor

b harmonic minor   f♯ harmonic minor

c♯ harmonic minor   g♯ harmonic minor

d♯ harmonic minor   a♯ harmonic minor

d harmonic minor   g harmonic minor

c harmonic minor   f harmonic minor

b♭ harmonic minor   e♭ harmonic minor

a♭ harmonic minor

IV. Write the ascending and descending forms of melodic minor scales with key signatures

a melodic minor

e melodic minor

b melodic minor

f♯ melodic minor

c♯ melodic minor

g♯ melodic minor

d♯ melodic minor

a♯ melodic minor

d melodic minor

g melodic minor

c melodic minor

f melodic minor

b♭ melodic minor

e♭ melodic minor

a♭ melodic minor

Homework 15

I. Identify and notate the requested notes. The first problem is done.

1. Dominant in g 2. Subdominant in d♯ 3. Supertonic in a 4. Leading tone in b♭ 5. Tonic in c♯

D

6. Submediant in e 7. Subdominant in f   8. Mediant in d   9. Leading tone in a♭ 10. Subdominant in g♯

11. Supertonic in e♭   12. Dominant in f♯ 13. Leading tone in c♯ 14. Subdominant in c 15. Dominant in a

II. Identify the minor key, write the key signature and notate the note in both staves.

1. F♯ is mediant   2. C is submediant   3. Eb is subdominant   4. C♯ is dominant 5. A♯ is leading tone

Key: _d♯_

6. B♭ is the subdominant 7. E is the submediant 8. G is the mediant 9. A is the subdominant 10. F is the dominant

Key:

11. A♭ is the subdom   12. D♭ is the subdom 13. B is the mediant 14. C is the supertonic 15. F is the submed

Key:_____

III. Write out the descending minor scale using key signatures

d♯ harmonic minor

e harmonic minor

g♯ natural minor

f harmonic minor

d melodic minor

c♯ natural minor

b♭ harmonic minor

Chapter Ten: Intervals

I. What is an interval and why do we care?

An interval is the distance between two notes. Intervals are the building blocks of scales and chords and are essential for a deeper understanding of music theory.

II. Calculating interval size

Interval size is easily determined by looking at the musical staff. Unisons are on the same line or space. Unisons share the same note name such as E and E.

U   U

Figure 10.1 Examples of unisons

The interval of a second is found between two notes that are on adjacent lines to spaces of the musical staff. They are one note apart. The interval is called a second because there are two notes involved, such as F and G, or B and C as in Figure 10.2.

2nd   2nd

Figure 10.2 Examples of seconds

The interval of a third is found between two notes that are on adjacent lines or adjacent spaces on the musical staff. The note F4 (first space on the treble clef) is a third away from A4 (second space on the treble clef). To calculate thirds we count up three notes from the bottom to the top note. From C up to E is a third: we count three notes up from C to E; C, D, E. Also C and E are on neighboring lines on the treble staff.

3rd   3rd

Figure 10.3 Examples of thirds

The interval of a fourth is one note bigger than a third. To calculate the interval of a fourth, start on any note and count up four notes including the starting note. If we start on F and count up four notes (F, G, A, B) we get to B. B is a fourth above F. On the staff we start on the note F, go up to the next space (a third), and then go one note higher to get to a fourth.

4th   4th

Figure 10.4 Examples of fourths

To find the interval of a fifth, skip a line or space on the staff between two notes. A fifth above the note F is found by counting up five notes (F, G, A, B, C). C is a fifth above F.

5th   5th

Figure 10.5 Examples of fifths

Sixths are one line or space above fifths. A sixth above the note F is found by counting up six notes (F, G, A, B, C, D) to D.

6th   6th

Figure 10.6 Examples of sixths

Sevenths skip two lines or spaces on the musical staff. A seventh can be found by counting up seven notes. A seventh above F (F, G, A, B, C, D, E) is the note E.

7th   7th

Figure 10.7 Examples of sevenths

Octaves are the next note higher or lower with the same name.

Figure 10.8 Examples of octaves

What is the size of this interval?

Exercise 10.1 What is the size of these intervals?

When calculating interval size only, as we have just done, we use only the letter names and no accidentals. This part of figuring out intervals is very simple and easy to do. Seconds will always be one note apart. Fifths will always have a space or line between the two notes on the staff. To get a fourth, we count up four notes. When counting up notes, we always include the top and bottom notes.

III. Interval quality: Perfect, major, minor, augmented and diminished

There are two parts to calculating intervals: size and quality. We have just learned how to calculate interval size. Keep in mind how simple and easy interval size is to calculate, as we tackle the more complex concept of interval quality.

Interval quality is classified as perfect, major, minor, or augmented or diminished (abbreviated P, M, m, A, d). When identifying an interval, we use a letter for quality (P, M, m, A, or d) followed by a number for size (except for unisons which use U for size). Interval size we have just learned to calculate in the above section. The basic interval qualities are perfect, major or minor. Some intervals are called perfect and others are called major or minor. Seconds, thirds, sixths and sevenths are called major or minor, while unisons, octaves, fourths and fifths are called perfect. An interval one half step bigger than major or perfect is augmented. An interval one half step smaller than a minor or perfect is called diminished. An interval two half steps bigger than major or perfect interval is called a doubly augmented interval. An interval two half steps smaller than a minor or perfect interval is called a doubly diminished interval. These parameters for interval quality are summarized in Figure 10.9.

Interval	← 1 HS smaller	← 1 HS smaller	Quality	1 HS bigger→	1 HS bigger→
U, 8, 4, 5	diminished		Perfect		Augmented
2, 3, 6, 7	diminished	minor		Major	Augmented

Figure 10.9 Interval quality

We will learn three methods for calculating interval quality.

IV. Calculating interval quality: Method 1, inversions

The first and one of the fastest methods used to calculate interval quality employs a few intervals as anchors. We learn the quality of anchor intervals and know them very well. To find larger and more complicated intervals we invert or alter the anchor intervals. We'll learn how to do interval inversions next.

How to do interval inversions

When we invert an interval we turn it upside down. What was on the bottom ends up on top. To do this we keep one note the same and move the other up or down by an octave. This can be understood clearly by looking at an example.

If we begin with the notes C and E, we see they are a third apart (C, D, E); they are on adjacent lines in the treble clef (C4 and E4). To invert we'll keep the E where it is and bring the C4 up an octave to C5. Now E is on the bottom and C is on the top. If we count up from E (E, F, G, A, B, C) we see that the inversion has created a different interval, the interval of the sixth.

Figure 10.10 Inversion of C4 and E4

Which note do we move and which do we keep the same? It doesn't matter, the answer will be the same, but if we retain the C and moved the E down an octave it would use ledger lines. We chose to move the C up in order to have both notes within the staff.

When inverting intervals the size changes: seconds invert to sevenths, thirds to sixths, fourths to fifths, and unisons to octaves. When inverting intervals the quality also changes: major intervals invert to minor intervals, perfect intervals invert to perfect, and augmented intervals invert to diminished. See Figure 10.11 for a summary of these qualities and how they are inverted.

	Interval			Interval
Size	Second	Inverts to		Seventh
	Third			Sixth
	Fourth			Fifth
	Unison			Octave
Quality	Major	Inverts to		Minor
	Perfect			Perfect
	Augmented			Diminished

Figure 10.11 Inversions of intervals

This will get clearer as we work through some examples.

Seconds and sevenths

We'll start with seconds because they are easy to count. One half step is a minor second (m2). Seconds invert to sevenths and minor intervals invert to major intervals. So a minor second will invert to a major seventh (M7).

    m2   M7   m2   M7

Figure 10.12 Minor seconds inverting to major sevenths

A major second (M2) has two half steps and inverts to a minor seventh (m7).

    M2   m7   M2   m7

Figure 10.13 Major second inverts to minor seventh

If a minor second gets one half step smaller it becomes a diminished second (d2). To make C to D♭ (m2) smaller, we can raise the C to C♯ or lower the D♭ to D♭♭. Either way we still have a second, as there are two notes involved, C and D. There are zero half steps between C♯ and D♭ and this is called a diminished second (d2). A diminished second sounds like a unison but is written on adjacent lines and spaces. It will invert to an augmented seventh.

Figure 10.14 Diminished second inverts to augmented seventh

If we are asked to identify an interval which we can see is a seventh (on the staff the two notes skip two lines or spaces), we can first invert it to an interval of a second, calculate the size of the second, then finally reinvert it back to get the quality of the seventh.

Figure 10.15 A seventh C4 to B4, invert to calculate the second, then reinvert to seventh

Augmented intervals invert to diminished intervals. In Figure 10.16 is an example of a seventh. We invert it to a second and then can easily see that it is a d2, C♯ to D♭. The two notes are on adjacent lines and spaces but they are enharmonic, they sound the same, and there are no half steps between them. This means the original interval was an augmented 7th (A7).

Figure 10.16 D♭4 up to C♯5 inverts to C♯5 to D♭5

So you can see even complex large intervals such as sevenths are easy to calculate as seconds. Just remember to invert back to sevenths to get the larger answer.

What is the size of this interval?   Create the interval above the given note.

Exercise 10. 2 Identify and create seconds and sevenths, size only

What is the size of this interval?   Create the interval above the given note.

                                                                        M2   M7

Exercise 10. 3 Identify and create seconds and sevenths, size and quality

Thirds and sixths

There are major thirds on three white notes: C F G. This means that a third on the white notes (no accidentals) above any of these three notes creates a major third interval. The rest of the white note thirds are minor thirds (D, E, A, B). By knowing that major thirds are on three notes (which ones? C, F, and G), we can also know the rest of the thirds. The thirds on the rest of the white notes are minor thirds. Which are minor thirds? D, E, A, B.

And the relationship is the same if we add the same accidentals to both of these notes. If C4 to E4 is a M3, then C♯4 to E♯4 is also a M3. And C♭♭4 to E♭♭4 is also a M3.

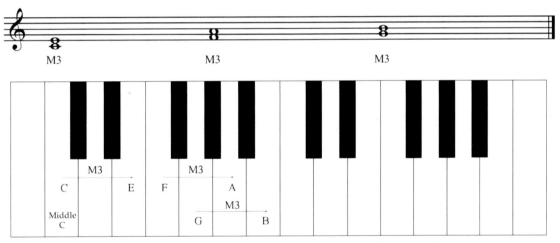

Figure 10. 17 The major thirds on C, F, and G. Notation and keyboard.

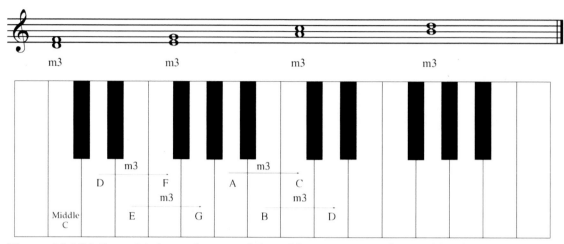

Figure 10.18 Minor thirds on the rest of the white notes, notation and keyboards

What is the size of this interval?   Create the interval above the given note.

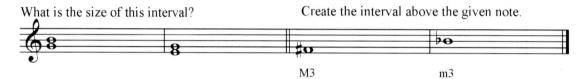

Exercise 10.4 Identify and create thirds?

Thirds invert to sixths. If we know our white note M3 (C, F, G) and m3 (the rest of them) we can easily invert to find the m6 and M6. F up to A is a M3. When we invert it, we have A up to F, a m6 as shown in Figure 10.19.

Figure 10.19 M3 and m3 inverting to m6 and M6

What if one of the notes has an accidental and the other doesn't?
When figuring out thirds with an accidental on only one note, take away the accidental, and figure out the white note interval. Then add the accidental back, and be clear if the interval has gotten bigger or smaller than with white note interval alone. Be visual; use your hands to show the white note intervals, than add the accidentals, one at a time, to see how the interval has changed. For example, if the problem is to calculate the interval from D♭4 to F♯4, take away both accidentals to calculate the white note interval, D up to F. We know this is a m3 (the bottom note isn't C, F, or G). Then add the accidentals back in one at a time. D to F is a m3. D♭ to F? Did it get bigger or smaller? D is on the bottom and D♭ lowers the note, so the interval got bigger and is now a M3. D♭ to F is a M3. Then add the F♯. Did the interval get bigger or smaller? F is on the top and was raised so the

interval got bigger. So if D♭ to F is a M3, D♭ to F♯ is one half step bigger or an augmented third (A3).

Figure 10.20 D♭4 to F♯4 accidentals added one at a time.

If there is confusion, take away the accidentals, until you can easily calculate the quality of the third. Then add the accidentals one at a time, taking care to note if the interval increases in size or decreases. Visualize the interval each time, as it is easy to make mistakes. If in the above example the accidentals were reversed D♯4 to F♭4, the answer would be completely different, a ddd3.

What is the size of this interval?   Create the interval above the given note.

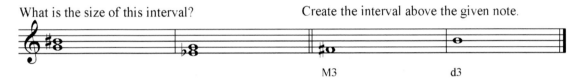

Exercise 10.5 Identify and create thirds and sixths with varying accidentals.

What is the size of this interval?   Create the interval above the given note.

Exercise 10.6 Identify and create seconds, thirds, sixths or sevenths.

Unison and Octave

Unisons are easy because they are on the same line or space. If they are the same note they are a perfect unison. Perfect unisons invert to perfect octaves.

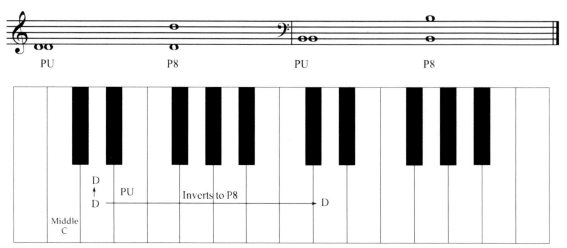

Figure 10.21 Perfect unison inverts to perfect octave, keyboard and notation.

If two notes share the same line or space on the staff, one has an accidental and the other doesn't, the two notes are a half step apart, and they are an augmented unison. This inverts to a diminished octave.

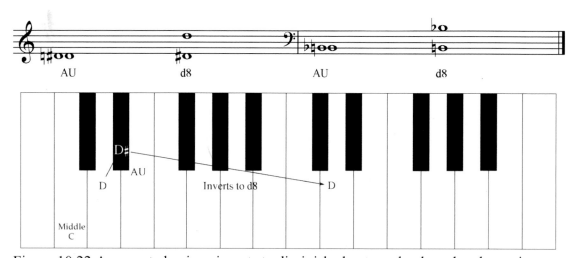

Figure 10.22 Augmented unison inverts to diminished octave, keyboard and notation.

If two notes are an octave apart plus one half step apart, they are an augmented octave. Since the distance between the two notes is greater than an octave, there are varying ideas of how to invert. If we change one note by an octave, the result is an augmented unison, but we haven't changed what was on the bottom so we have a reduction not an inversion.

There is no such thing as a diminished unison, except in imaginary worlds. You can't have an interval smaller than zero half steps (though some theorists will debate this).

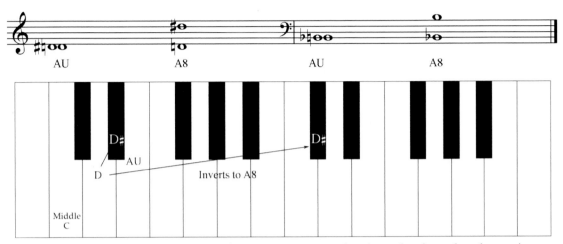
Figure 10.23 Augmented octave reduces to augmented unison, keyboard and notation

What is the size of this interval?   Create the interval above the given note.

Exercise 10.7 Identify and create unisons and octaves with varying accidentals.

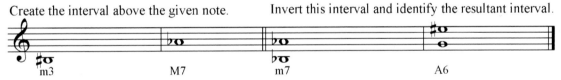

Create the interval above the given note.   Invert this interval and identify the resultant interval.

Exercise 10.8 Identify and create and invert intervals; U 2, 3, 6, 7, 8

Fourths and fifths
Fourths and fifths are perfect if they share the same accidental or have no accidental, unless the bottom note is F or B. A perfect fourth above D is G (D, E, F, G). A perfect fifth above E is B (E, F, G, A, B).

Figure 10.24 Perfect fourths and fifths with same accidental or no accidentals

To create a perfect fourth (P4) above F, the top note has to be reduced by a half step. F up to B♭ is a P4. A P4 above F♯ is B. F to B is an augmented fourth (A4).

A4   P4   P4

Figure 10.25 Interval F to B, an A4, F to B♭, a P4, F♯ to B, a P4

To create a perfect fifth (P5) above B, the top note must be raised a half step, or the B lowered to B♭.

d5   P5   P5

Figure 10.26 B to F, d5; B♭ to F, P5; B to F♯, P5

If two notes form a fourth or fifth and one has an accidental, first take away the accidental to calculate the white key interval. Then add the accidentals back in, one at a time. When figuring out the interval from E♭4 to B4, first look at E4 to B4. Neither note has an accidental and the bottom note is not F or B. So E4 up to B4 is a P5. Then add the E♭, which increases the interval size by one HS, creating an A5.

interval got larger

?   P5   A5

Figure 10.27 E♭4 to B4, E4 to B4, P5

Create the interval above the given note.   Invert this interval and identify the resultant interval.

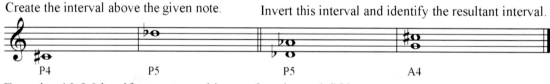

P4   P5   P5   A4

Exercise 10.9 Identify, create and invert fourths and fifths.

Create the interval above the given note.   Invert this interval and identify the resultant interval.

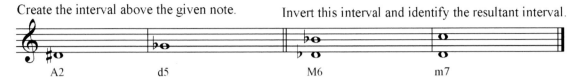

A2   d5   M6   m7

Exercise 10.10 Identify, create and invert all intervals

V. Calculating interval quality: Method 2: Key signatures, intervals above a tonic

Key signatures can be used to calculate interval quality. In a major scale every interval above the tonic is either M (2, 3, 6, 7) or perfect (4, 5, 8). In Figure 10.28 the notes of the C major scale are all major or perfect intervals above the tonic note C.

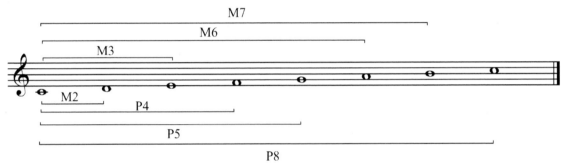

Figure 10.28 Major scale, every interval above the tonic is major or perfect

If you want to identify an interval, first calculate the size. Then use the bottom note as tonic and ask if the top note is in the key signature. If it is, then the interval will be a major or perfect interval. In Figure 10.29 all the top notes in the second measure are in the key of A major, so all the intervals are major or perfect (M6, M7, P4, P5).

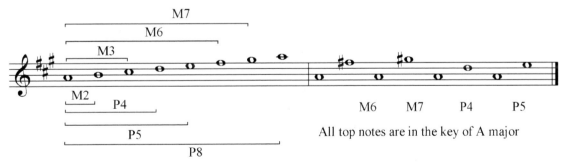

Figure 10.29 A4 to F♯5, in the key of A major, M6, the key signature has three sharps, F♯, C♯ and G♯

If the top note is not in the key of the bottom note, then we have to see if the interval has increased or decreased in size. When examining the interval from A to F, we first look at the key signature for A major which has three sharps, F♯, C♯, and G♯. F is not in the key signature for A major. A is 6 notes up to F (A, B, C, D, E, F) so the size of the interval is a sixth. A up to F♯ would have been a M6. We lower F♯ to F♮, and the interval gets smaller. So A up to F is m6.

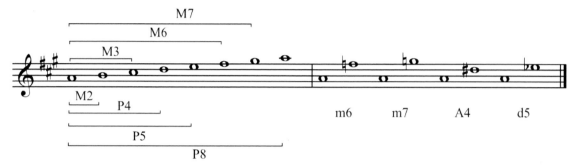

Figure 10.30 A4 to F5, F5 makes the interval smaller by one half step then A4 to F♯5, so the interval is a m6.

VI. Calculating interval quality: Method 3: Counting half steps
The slowest and the least accurate method of calculating interval quality involves a tedious process of counting half steps. When we count half steps, we must have the music keyboard in front of us (or in our minds) to get the whole steps and half steps in the right places. While we can all theoretically count to 12, in practice, many students count very slowly, lose track and make mistakes when using this method.

TT stands for tritone, three whole steps (tri means three) or 6 half steps. A tritone is called an A4 or a d5 depending on how it is notated. The chart in Figure 10.31 is not exhaustive, as there are many more possible intervals (A3, d4, d2, etc.).

Interval	Number of half steps
m2	1
M2	2
m3	3
M3	4
P4	5
TT or A4/d5	6
P5	7
m6 /A5	8
M6	9
m7	10
M7	11
P8	12

Figure 10.31 Intervals and number of half steps

To calculate the number of half steps in diminished or augmented intervals increase (for augmented intervals) or decrease (for diminished intervals) the number of half steps by one.

VII. Getting fast at calculating interval size and quality.
Whichever method you use, you must be confident and quick for it to be of use musically. Don't use the counting half step method if you want to be fast.

Anchor intervals and white key intervals
Remember anchor intervals if you use the inversion method. Major thirds on what three notes? C, F, and G. The rest are minor thirds. Invert to find sixths. Seconds are easy to calculate, invert to find sevenths. If you memorize the white key intervals you will have a lot of power in knowing your intervals.

Key signatures
Know your key signatures very well if you use the key signature method. To know the key signatures, learn the Circle of Fifths and be able to draw it within one minute (including major and minor scales and all enharmonic keys)

VIII. Compound intervals
Compound intervals are intervals that are larger than an octave. Add the number seven to the smaller interval (less than an octave) to get the correct number for the compound interval. Compound intervals have the same qualities as their reduced counterparts. An octave and a step (a second) is called a ninth (7+2). In Figure 10.32 a M2, D4 to E4, becomes a M9 when we add an octave, D4 to E5.

Figure 10.32 Ninths, octave plus second

An octave plus a third is called a tenth. In Figure 10.33 a M3, D4 to F♯4, becomes a M10 when an octave is added, D4 to F♯5. To calculate the compound interval, retain the quality (M or m) and add 7 to the interval size.

M10   M3+8va   m10   m10+8va   M10   M3+8va   m10   m3+8va

Figure 10.33 Tenths, octave plus third

An octave plus a fourth is called an eleventh. In Figure 10.34 a P4 (D4 to G4) becomes a P11 (D4 to G5). A dim4, G4 to C♭5, becomes a d11 when an octave is added (maintain quality and add 7 to the size of the reduced interval to calculate the compound interval from G4 to C♭6).

P11   P4+8va   d11   d11+8va   P11   P11+8va   A11   A11+8va

Figure 10.34 Elevenths, octave plus fourth

An octave plus a fifth is called a twelfth.

P12   P5+8va   d12   d5+8va   P12   P5+8va   A12   A5+8va

Figure 10.35 Twelfths, octave plus fifth

An octave an a sixth is called a thirteenth.

M13   M6+8va   m13   m6+8va   d13   d6+8va   A13   A6+8va

Figure 10.36 Thirteenths, octave plus sixth

An octave plus a seventh is called a fourteenth.

M14   M7+8va   m14   m7+8va   d14   d7+8va   A14   A7+8va

Figure 10.37 Fourteenths, octave plus seventh

Two octaves is abbreviated 15va (a fifteenth, though no one calls it that).

P15   P8+8va   d15   d8+8va   P15   P8+8va   A15   A8+8va

Figure 10.38 Two octaves

What is the size of the interval?.   Create this interval.

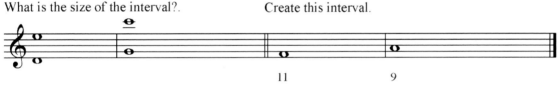

11   9

Exercise 10.11 Identify and create compound intervals, size only

IX. Reducing compound intervals to calculate interval quality

Compound intervals can be reduced to less than an octave by subtracting the octave. This simple process makes the interval smaller by one octave by changing the octave of one of the two notes. If we want to determine the interval between the two notes D♯4 and A5, we would start by bringing A5 down to A4 or bringing D♯4 up to D♯5. Either way the interval distance is the same. Then it is easy to calculate the distance between the two notes, a d5. Unlike inversions, the two notes don't switch what is on top or bottom. The same note remains on the bottom and top as when you began. You can do this numerically by subtracting seven from the compound interval size.

?   d5+8va   d12   (5 + 7 = 12)

Figure 10.39 Reducing compound intervals

Interval quality of compound intervals is the same as that of the reduced interval. So instead of calculating interval quality of a compound interval, reduce it to within an octave, use one of the above methods to calculate the interval quality then add seven back to interval size to get the original size and quality of the compound interval. Retain the quality when adding seven to the reduced interval to get the quality of the compound interval.

For the interval from D♭4 up to G♭5, we see that the interval is compound, that it is greater than an octave. To identify it, first reduce the interval to within an octave by bringing the G♭5 down to G♭4. Both D♭ and G♭ have the same accidental so we can ignore it in figuring out the interval size and quality. We see that D up to G is a fourth (D, E, F, G). D is on the bottom and it isn't F or B, so D up to G is a P4. D♭ up to G♭ is also a P4. To get to the original interval, move G♭4 back up to G♭5. Add seven to the interval size (4 +7 equals 11), and retain the quality, perfect. D♭4 up to G♭5 is a P11.

?   P4+8va   P11   (4 + 7 = 11) retain quality

Figure 10.40 Compound interval, reduced by octave, identify the interval, expand out to original interval

What is this interval?.   Create this interval.

                                                                   M10   P12

Exercise 10.12 Calculate and create interval size and quality of compound intervals

Review of Intervals

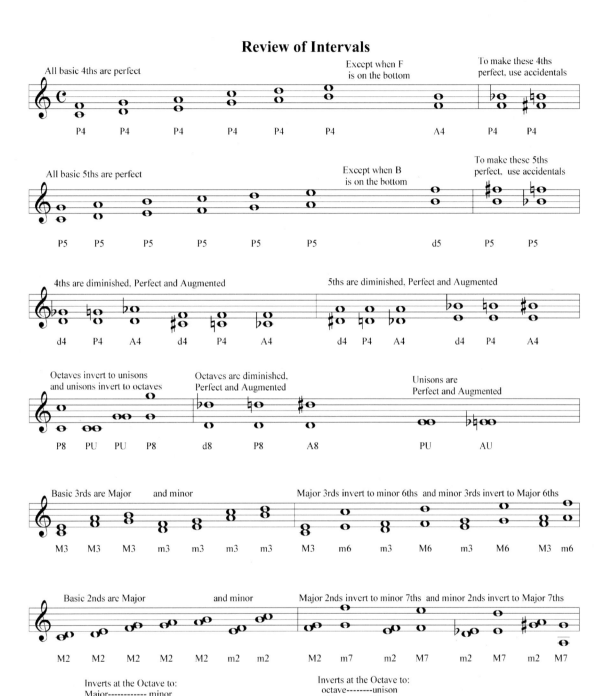

Homework 16

I. Identify the interval size.

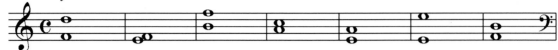

II. Write the given interval **above** the indicated note

2   4   3   6   4   7   U   8   5

III. Write the given interval **below** the indicated note

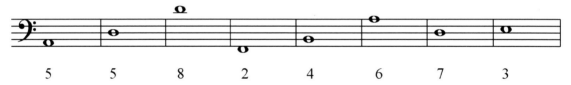

5   5   8   2   4   6   7   3

IV. Identify the interval size, invert it, then identify the inverted interval.

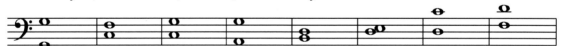

V. Identify the size and quality of the following intervals.

Homework 17

I. Identify the interval size and quality.

II. Write the given interval **above** the indicated note

M2   m3   P4   P5   P5   m6   M2   M7   AU

III. Write the given interval **below** the indicated note

M3   d3   P8   M2   P4   M6   m7   A8

IV. Identify the interval size and quality, invert it, then identify the inverted interval.

V. Identify the size and quality of the following intervals.

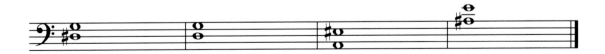

Homework 18

I. Identify the interval and quality

II. Write the given interval above the indicated note

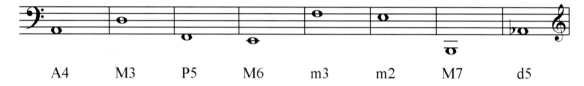

A4   M3   P5   M6   m3   m2   M7   d5

III. Write the given interval below the indicated note

d5   m6   P4   P5   M3   M2   m6   M2

IV. Identify the interval size and quality, invert it, then identify the inverted interval.

V. Reduce the compound interval to within an octave, identify both intervals.

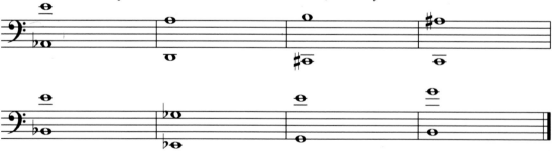

Chapter Eleven: Triads

I. What is a chord?

Notes, scales, keys, and chords can all share the same name. The note C is one tone, the C scale has 7 tones, the key of C is a collection of pitches that contain the C scale and the chord C is composed of three notes C, E, and G. A chord is created when more than two or more pitches are sounded simultaneously. A three note chord is called a triad. On the musical staff they occupy adjacent lines or spaces with the notes a third apart. On the piano they are played on every other note. The D minor chord is composed of the notes D F and A. Figure 11.1 shows some examples of different triads.

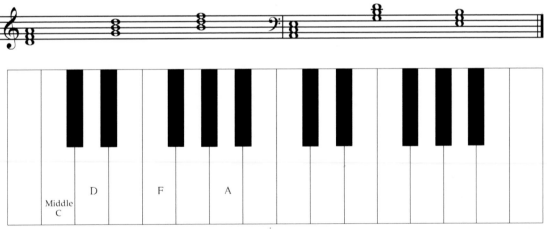

Figure 11.1 Triads on staff and keyboard.

Each note of the chord has a label. The root is the bottom note, the third is the middle note, and the fifth is the top note. These names come from the scale. If we created a scale starting on the bottom note of the chord, the middle note is the third note of the scale and the top note is the fifth note of the scale.

Figure 11.2 A C major scale; C E and G are the 1, 3 and 5

Four Triads

There are four types of three note chords: major, minor, augmented and diminished. Each is composed of specific types of thirds.

II. Major Triad

The major triad is composed of a M3 on the bottom and a m3 on the top and has a happy sound. Figure 11.3 shows some examples of major triads.

Figure 11.3 Major triads

If we play only white notes, there are three major triads with the bottom notes being C, F, and G. This corresponds to the M3 intervals on the same three notes.

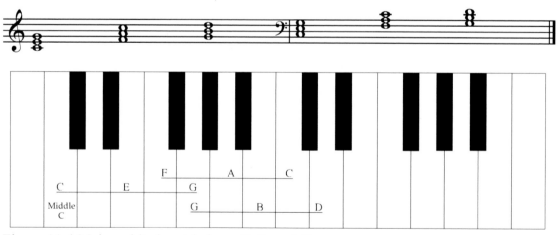

Figure 11.4 Major white key triads on C, F, and G

III. Minor Triad

The minor triad is composed of a m3 on the bottom and a M3 on the top.

If we play only white notes, there are three minor triads with the bottom notes being D, E, and A.

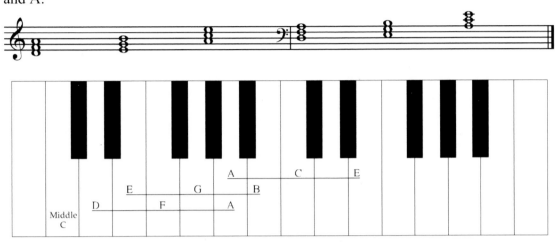

Figure 11.5 Three minor white key triads on D, E, and A

IV. Diminished triad

The diminished triad is composed of a m3 on the bottom and a m3 on top.

Figure 11.6 Diminished triads

If we play only white notes, there is only one diminished triad, the B diminished triad. B is the bottom note, or the root, of the chord.

Figure 11.7 Diminished white key triad on B

V. Augmented triad

The augmented triad is composed of a M3 on the bottom and M3 on top.
If we play only white notes, there are no augmented triads. To create an augmented triad we must add accidentals.

Figure 11.8 Augmented triads

VI. Comparing the four triads

If we compare the intervals between the bottom and top notes in the four triads, we see that the M and m triads both have a P5 interval between the bottom and top notes. The diminished triad is one half step smaller, a d5, and the augmented triad is one half step larger, an A5.

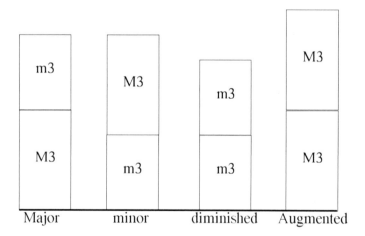

Figure 11.9 The four triads are composed of major and minor thirds

Exercise 11.1 Identify the triads

VII. How to create any chord
Starting on any note we can create any of the four chord types by using one of three methods: intervals, anchor chords or key signatures.

Using intervals to create chords
Using the intervals M3 and m3, the intervals that compose each of the four triads, we can create any chord. For example a major triad on the note C is created by starting on C, going up a M3 from C to the note E, then a m3 up from E to the note G. So playing the notes C E G creates a major triad on C.

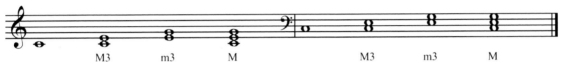

Figure 11.10 A triad on C

For a minor triad, we start on C, go up a m3 to the note E♭, then go up a M3 to the note G. Notice both the major and minor triad on C share the bottom and top notes, C and G. Only the middle note is different.

Figure 11.11 C major and C minor chords

For a diminished triad we start on the note C, ascend a m3 to the note E♭, and then ascend another m3 to the note G♭. Notice this is a half step below the top note of the C major and minor triads.

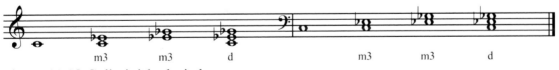

Figure 11.12 C diminished triad

For the augmented triad, begin on C, ascend a M3 to the note E, and then ascend another M3 to the note G♯. Notice the top note is a half step higher than the top note for the M and m triads.

Figure 11.13 C augmented triad

In Figure 11.14 four triads built on the root C are compared.

Figure 11.14 The comparison for all the four triads on C

Create a triad.

Exercise 11.2 Create triads using intervals

We can easily create any triad on any note by knowing how to create major and minor thirds.

VIII. Using anchor chords to create any chord

There are major triads on what three white note chords? C, F, and G. The same interval relationships are maintained if there are no accidentals or all the accidentals are the same. That means we can also spell major triads on C♯, F♯, and G♯. A major triad on C is CEG, so a major triad on C♯ is C♯E♯G♯. And a major triad on C♭ is C♭, E♭, G♭.

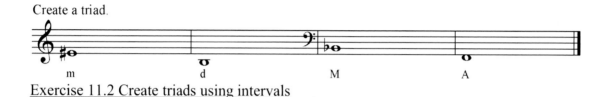

Figure 11.15 Major triads on C, C♯, C♭, C𝄪, and C♭♭

There are minor triads on all the other notes (except for B which is diminished). A minor triad on D is DFA. And this also makes it easy to spell a minor triad on D♭ which is D♭, F♭, A♭.

Figure 11.16 Minor triads on D, D♯, D♭, D𝄪, and D♭♭.

The diminished triad on B is BDF. So a diminished triad on B♭ would be B♭, D♭, F♭.

Figure 11.17 Diminished triad on B, B♭ and B𝄪

Create a triad.

Exercise 11.3 Notate chords with same accidentals or no accidentals.

To spell other chords, see below to transform one chord quality into another.

IX. How to change from one chord to another
By changing only one accidental in a three note chord, the chord is transformed into a different chord quality. For example if we know that a major chord on C is CEG. How do we spell a minor chord on C? We flat the third of the chord. Here is a list of how a change in one accidental can change the chord quality.

Major → minor ♭3
minor → Major ♯3
Major → Augmented ♯5
minor → diminished ♭5
Figure 11.18 One note changes in accidental and change of chord quality

Figure 11.19 Changes from M to m, m to M, M to A, m to d

Change each chord as indicated.

M   m   m   M   M   A   m   d

Exercise 11.4 Change the notated chords from M to m, m to M, M to A, m to d

Here is a more complete list of how to change one chord into another.

Major → minor ♭3
Major → Augmented ♯5
Major → diminished ♯1 or ♭3, ♭5
minor → Major ♯3
minor → diminished ♭5
minor → augmented ♭1 or ♯3, ♯5
diminished → Major ♭1 or ♯3, ♯5
diminished → minor ♯5
diminished → Augmented ♭1, ♯5 or ♯3, x5
Augmented → Major ♭5
Augmented → minor ♯1 or ♭5, ♭3
Augmented → diminished ♯1, ♭5 or ♭3, ♭♭5

Figure 11.20 Changing chords by changing multiple accidentals

Start to know your chords by learning the transformations that require only one change of accidental as shown in Figure 11.18 above. Later you can learn the list shown in Figure 11.20.

X. Using key signatures to spell chords
Using the key signatures, we can spell all the major and minor triads by using the tonic of each key. To name the notes of a major triad with D♭ as the root would examine the key of D♭ major for the appropriate accidentals. The key signature for D♭ major has 5 flats, B♭ E♭, A♭, D♭, G♭. The triad on D is DFA. If we add the flats from the D♭ key signature we create the D♭ F A♭ chord, which is the D♭ tonic triad and is major.

M

Figure 11.21 Major triad on D♭ using a key signature

XI. How to get faster at creating chords
To spell triads quickly it is helpful to drill the spelling of the triads in either of the
following ways.
Say and write the triads until you know them all perfectly, forwards and backwards,
without thinking.

CEG, DFA, EGB, FAC, GBD, ACE, BDF, CEG
Exercise 11.5 Spell triads in thirds: say these out loud until they can be recited without
looking and without hesitation

Another drill is to practice the triads in ascending thirds

CEG, EGB, GBD, BDF, DFA, FAC, ACE, CEG
Figure 11.22 White note triads

After these are easily and quickly spoken and written, then practice spelling specific
triads. For example, spell all the major triads on white keys. Knowing the anchor keys is
very helpful. Major triads are on which three notes? C, F, and G. The rest are minor with
the exception of B, which is diminished.
To make a minor chord major, we raise the third. To make the diminished chord major,
we raise the third and the fifth.
Then we can spell all the white key major chords without difficulty.

CEG, DF♯A, EG♯B, FAC, GBD, AC♯E, BD♯F♯, CEG
Figure 11.23 Major triads

Notate all the white note triads as indicated.

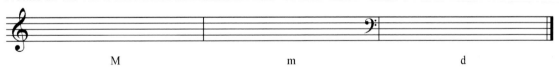

M   m   d

Exercise 11.6 Drills creating all white note root M m A or d triads

XII. How to build chords above a bass
So far we have created triads above a note that was the root of the chord.

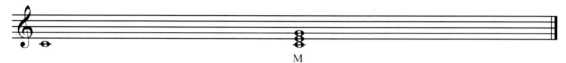

Figure 11.24 C as root, major triad

We can also create a triad with the given note as the third or fifth of the chord. If the given note is the third of the chord, stack the chord by putting a third above the given note, and a third below the given note.

To create a major chord from the third of the chord, the middle note, build a m3 above and a M3 below the note.

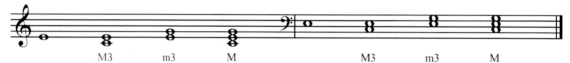

Figure 11.25 Building a major chord around E, the third of the chord

We can create a chord where the given note is the fifth of the chord by notating a third down from the given note, then an additional third down. To create a major chord starting from the fifth of the chord, notate a m3 downwards, then another M3 downward.

Figure 11.26 Building a major chord around G, the fifth of the chord

For the given chord quality, create the chord by building thirds above and below the given note and then adding in appropriate accidentals. For example if the given note is E and it is the third of a minor triad, first write the third below, C, and the third above, G. To create a minor triad, there is a m3 on the bottom and a M3 on the top. Go a m3 down from E, or 3 half steps. The note is C♯, so add a ♯ in front of the C. Then go up a M3 from E or 4 half steps. The note is G♯ so add a ♯ before the G. A minor triad around the note E, which is the third of a chord, is C♯ E G♯. This is shown in Figure 11.27.

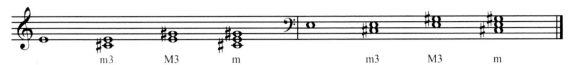

Figure 11.27 Build a minor triad with E as the given note, the third of the chord.

In Figure 11.28 the problem is to build a major triad around the note C, which is the third of chord.

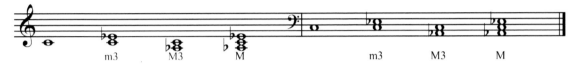

Figure 11.28 Build a major triad with C as the given note, the third of the chord.

In Figure 11.29 the problem is to build a major triad with A as the fifth of the chord.

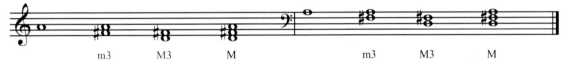

Figure 11.29 Build a major triad with A as the given note, the fifth of the chord.

In Figure 11.30 a diminished chord is built with F♯ as the third of the chord.

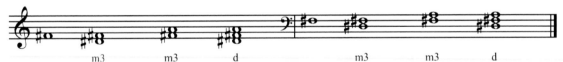

Figure 11.30 Build a diminished triad with F♯ as the given note, the third of the chord.

In Figure 11.31 an augmented triad is created below the fifth of the chord, B.

Figure 11.31 Build an augmented triad with B as the given note, the fifth of the chord.

Notate a triad
above the root.

Notate chord,
given note is the third.

Notate chord,
given note is the fifth.

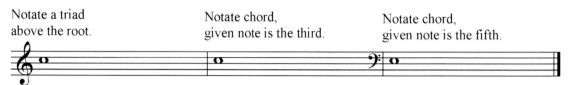

Exercise 11.7 Create chords with given note as root, third, or fifth of chord, no quality

Notate a M triad
above the root

Notate m chord,
given note is the third.

Notate d chord,
given note is the fifth.

Exercise 11.8 Create specific chord types with given note as root, third, and fifth of chord

Homework 19

I.   Write in the notes for the specified chords - the given note is the root

II. Identify the chords (M, m, A, d)

Homework 20

I. Write in the notes for the specified chords - the given note is the root

II Write in the notes for the specified chords - the given note is the third

III. Write in the notes for the specified chords - the given note is the fifth

IV. Identify the chords (M, m, A, d)

Chapter Twelve: Harmonized Scales

I. Harmonized Major Scales

If we take any major scale and put a three note chord on every scale degree, we have added harmony to the scale and have created a harmonized scale. The harmonized C major scale is shown in Figure 12.1.

Harmonized C Major scale

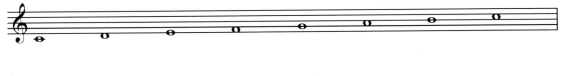

Figure 12.1 C major scale and C major harmonized scale

On each scale degree a chord is created. What is the quality of each chord? The pattern of chord qualities for every harmonized major scale is the same. M m m M M m d.

Harmonized C Major scale

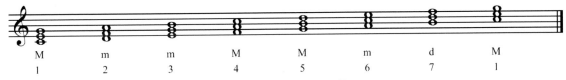

Figure 12.2 C major harmonized scale and chord quality

The patterns can help us remember the chord qualities of the harmonized scale. There are major chords on C, F, and G. These chords are built on the first, fourth, and fifth scale degrees in the C major scale as shown in Figure 12.3.

Harmonized C Major scale

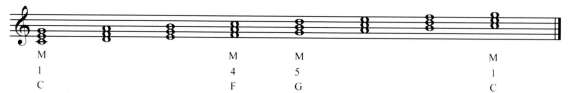

Figure 12.3 Harmonized C major scale, chord quality and numbers on C F and G

This is true for every major scale – the chords on the first, the fourth and the fifth scale degrees in a major key are always major.

Of the remaining triads, all of them are minor except for the triad on B, which is diminished.

Harmonized C Major scale

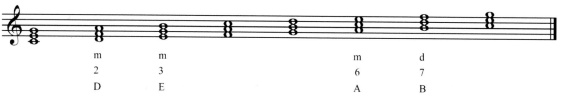

Figure 12.4 Harmonized C major scale, chord quality and numbers on D, E, A, B

For every major scale the chords on the second, third and sixth scale degrees are minor and the chord on the seventh scale degree is diminished.

Harmonized C Major scale

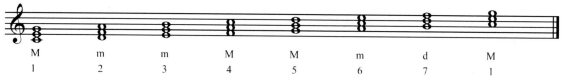

Figure 12.5 Harmonized C major scale, chord quality and numbers

These patterns are the same for any major scale.

Harmonized G Major scale

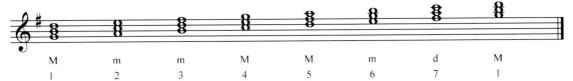

Figure 12.6 Harmonized G major scale, chord quality and numbers

II. Why learn harmonized scales?

The set of chords created by the harmonized scale are the chords that will harmonize the music of any particular key. The chords C, Dm, Em, F, G, Am, and B° are the chords that make up the C harmonized scale and are the chords that would best harmonize a melody in C major.

By knowing the harmonized scale patterns we can begin to understand music and how it functions.

III. Roman numerals and chord function

Roman numerals are assigned to each chord of the harmonized scale. If a chord is major a capital Roman numeral is used. For example in the C major harmonized scale the first chord is C major and the Roman numeral I is used. The fourth chord is F major so the Roman numeral IV is used and the fifth chord is G, which is also major so V is used. For minor chords, lower case Roman numerals are used. In the C harmonized scale the Roman numerals ii, iii, and vi designate the Dm, Em, and Am chords respectively. Diminished chords use lower case Roman numerals with a superscript circle. For the B° chord in the harmonized C scale, the Roman numeral vii° is used.

Harmonized D Major scale

Figure 12.7 Harmonized D major scale, Roman numerals, chord quality and numbers

Again this pattern is true for every major key.

$E = V$

$Cm = vi$

Harmonized F Major scale

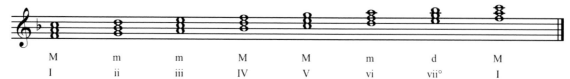

M	m	m	M	M	m	d	M
I	ii	iii	IV	V	vi	vii°	I

Figure 12.8 Harmonized F major scale with Roman numerals

Label harmonized A Major scale with Roman Numerals

Exercise 12.1 Label harmonized scale in A with Roman numerals

IV. What do Roman numerals have to do with chord function?

In any key we can understand the function of a chord once we assign Roman numerals to the chord. The G major chord has a different function in the key of G major when compared to its function in the key of C major. In G, the G major chord is the home chord and when we hear it, the music sounds finished and complete.

Figure 12.9 Chorale ending on tonic

However in the key of C, the chord G functions as the V and if we land on the V chord it doesn't sound like we are done. Instead the chord functions as a bridge leading us to the final chord, C.

C: V   V____   I

Figure 12.10 Chorale that rests on the V, then leads to the I

If we analyze the music that we enjoy, observing the patterns of chords and their Roman numerals, we can begin to understand how the music is constructed and how it functions.

V. The Harmonized scale and scale degree names

Each chord of the harmonized scale uses the same name as the notes of the scale: tonic, supertonic, mediant, subdominant, dominant, submediant, leading tone. The pattern of chord quality is Major, minor, minor, Major, Major, minor, diminished.

Harmonized E♭ Major scale

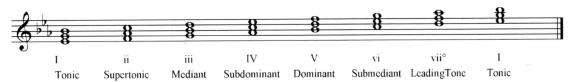

| I | ii | iii | IV | V | vi | vii° | I |
| Tonic | Supertonic | Mediant | Subdominant | Dominant | Submediant | LeadingTone | Tonic |

Figure 12.11 Harmonized scale with Roman numerals and scale degree names

The first and most important chord in any key is the tonic chord, the next most important chord is the dominant, and the third most important chord is the subdominant. These three chords, tonic, dominant, and subdominant, I, IV, and V chords, are the primary triads in every key. It is helpful for all musicians to learn these three chords in every key.

We can also use the Circle of Fifths to find the primary triads. Surrounding each tonic key are the two chords that are the subdominant (IV) and dominant (V). The subdominant is to the left and dominant is to the right. If we look at the key of C on the Circle of Fifths, F is immediately to the left and G is to the right of C. F is the subdominant of C, and G is the dominant of C. If we start at the key of A, D is to the left of A and E is to the right of A, and D is the subdominant of A and E is the dominant. The Circle of Fifths can be used to find subdominants and dominants for all major and minor keys.

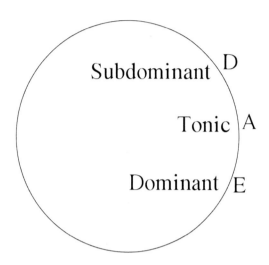

Figure 12.12 The Circle of Fifths with A, D, and E showing tonic, subdominant and dominant

Actually 6 of the 7 chords of the harmonized scale surround the tonic on the Circle of Fifths with minor keys showing the minor chords on the inside of the circle.

Notate the primary triads in the key of B major and D♭ major.

Exercise 12.2 What are the primary triads in these keys?

We can find the quality of the chords in any key using our understanding of key signatures from the Circle of Fifths and the harmonized scale. For example if we want to know the quality of a chord spelled A♭ C E♭, we look at the first note of the chord as the tonic of a major key, A♭ major. What is the key signature for A♭ major? Four flats. What are they? B♭, E♭, A♭, D♭. Are the notes A♭ C E♭ all in the key of A♭ major? Yes they are, so the chord is the same as the tonic triad and is major. Using this method we don't have to count half steps or calculate thirds, we only use the key signatures.

I

Tonic

Figure 12.13 A♭ major chord and key signature of A♭ major

Assume the first chord to be tonic. What is the chord quality and roman numeral of the second chord?

Exercise 12.3 What is the quality of the chord using key signatures

VI. Harmonized Minor Scales

The minor scales can also be harmonized resulting in a pattern of chord quality for each scale degree. If we harmonize the natural minor scale the pattern of chords on each scale degree is m d M m m M M. This is shown in Figure 12.14.

Harmonized A minor scale

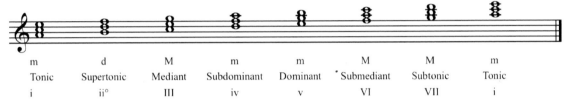

m	d	M	m	m	M	M	m
Tonic	Supertonic	Mediant	Subdominant	Dominant	Submediant	Subtonic	Tonic
i	ii°	III	iv	v	VI	VII	i

Figure 12.14 Harmonized natural minor scale with quality and Roman numerals.

Most often the harmonized minor scale uses the harmonic minor scale with the raised seventh scale degree resulting in a change of harmony on two chords. The minor v of the natural minor scale becomes a major chord, and the chord on the seventh is built on the raised seventh and is diminished.

Harmonized A harmonic minor scale

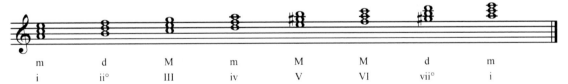

m	d	M	m	M	M	d	m
i	ii°	III	iv	V	VI	vii°	i

Figure 12.15 Harmonized harmonic minor scale

VII. Chords and inversion, figured bass numbers and Roman numerals

When a chord is played with a note other than the root in the bass, it is in an inversion. Any chord can be played in an inversion. If the third is in the bass, it is in first inversion.

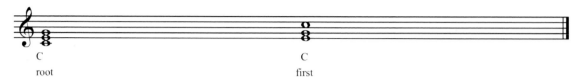

Figure 12.16 C major triad in root position and in first inversion

In the second chord of Figure 12.16, the same three notes of the C chord are still present, but the lowest note in the chord in no longer C, the root of the chord. The lowest note is E. In inversions, the top notes can be arranged in any order. To determine the inversion we only look at the lowest note.

If a C chord is played with G in the bass, this is called second inversion.

Figure 12.17 C chord in first and second inversions

When a chord is in an inversion, the Roman numeral is modified to show the inversion. If the chord is in first inversion, a 6 is added after the Roman numeral to show that there is an interval of a 6th above the bass note. Figure 12.18 shows the harmonized C major scale in root position and first inversion.

Harmonized C Major scale

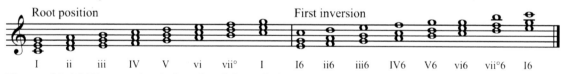

Figure 12.18 Harmonized chords of C scale in root position and first inversion

If the chord is in second inversion, the numbers 6/4 are added to the Roman numerals to indicate that the intervals of a sixth and a fourth are above the given bass. The use of numbers (6 and 6/4) comes from a Baroque system called Figured Bass.

Harmonized C Major scale

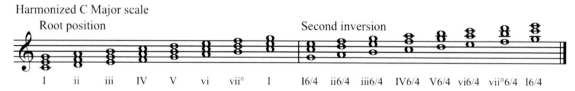

Figure 12.19 Harmonized chords of C scale in root position and second inversion

VIII. Seventh chords, Dominant seventh chords

If another third is stacked on a triad, this adds the seventh to the chord. The dominant chord is often played with an added seventh, though any chord can have a seventh.

In the key of C, the dominant is built on the chord G. If thirds are stacked above G, third, fifth and seventh, the notes G, B, D, and F are played. This is the dominant seventh in the key of C symbolized as the V7.

Figure 12.20 G7 chord in the key of C

The dominant seventh chord in any key functions to pull the listener strongly to the tonic chord.

Figure 12.21 Chorale with V7 I ending

IX. Using key signatures to compose chords for a song

By knowing the harmonized scale, composing a song in any key becomes simpler. First write the harmonized scale in the key. This will show the chords that will fit with any given scale or melody.

If we compose a song in the key of E major, the chords that we can use are E major, F♯ minor, G# minor, A major, B major, C♯ minor, and D♯ °.

Here is a melody in the key of E major.

Figure 12.22 Melody in E major

By choosing chords that support the melody at strong accents, the song can be harmonized.

Figure 12.23 Melody of figure 12.22 harmonized

Figure 12.24 shows an alternative way to harmonize the same melody.

Figure 12.24 Alternate harmonization

Create the chords on the given root.

Exercise 12.4 Create chords on given notes as root, M m A d

Create chord with given note as third.   Create a chord with given note as fifth

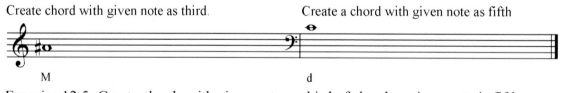

Exercise 12.5 Create chords with given note as third of chord or given note is fifth

Identify the root, the chord quality, and the inversion.

Exercise 12.6 Identify quality, root, inversion

X. Lead Sheet Chord Symbols

Another way chords can be written in music is by using lead sheet chord symbols. Chord symbols can be very simple for triads, or can use a variety of letters, numbers and symbols to represent more complex chords. In this chapter we have discussed triads and seventh chords in root position, first inversion, and second inversion. Below is a list showing common chord symbols for the triads and dominant seventh chords. Lead sheet chord symbols are placed above the staff and are used in pop, folk, jazz, and blues. Many books of music contain only the melody and lead sheet chords. This then leaves the interpretation of how to perform the rhythm accompaniment, up to the musician. The inversions use a slash to show what is in the bass.

	Major	Minor	Diminished	Augmented	Dominant seventh
Root position	C	Cm	C°	C+	C7
First inversion	C/E	Cm/E♭	C°/ E♭	C+/ E	C7/ E
Second inversion	C/G	Cm/G	C°/ G♭	C+/G♯	C7/G

Figure 12.25 Lead sheet chord symbols

Homework 21 – Final Review

I. Write out each harmonized scale. Label each chord with roman numerals (bottom) and lead sheet chord symbols (top).

    1. g harmonic minor   2. A♭ major

    3. g♯ natural minor   4. F♯ major

II In the given key, identify the chords by lead sheet chord symbol (above the staff) and roman numeral (below the staff).

    1. C major   2. A major   3. g minor

    4. B♭ major   5. f minor   6. B major

III. In the given key, notate the requested chord..Label with lead sheet chord symbols on top.

    1. G: V   2. a: V   3. C: ii   4. d: VI   5. e:iio   6. A: viio   7. Ab: iii   8. F♯: I   9. Db: IV   10. g: III

IV. Create the requested chord in the requested inversion.

    1. Gm, 1st inv 2. A, 2nd inv   3. B dim, root   4. D♯m, 1st inv   5. B, 2nd inv   6. F♯m, root   7. Gdim, 1st inv   8. Gb+, root

V. Notate the chords for the following progression. Label each chord with lead sheet chord symbols on top of the staff.

G: I   ii   IV   vi   V   iii   viio   2. Eb: I   V   ii   IV   ii   viio   vi

VI. Identify the inversion, root and quality of each chord

Root

inversion   —   —   —   —   —   —   —

quality   —   —   —   —   —   —   —

VII. Invert each chord as specified, then identify the quality and root.

ist inv   2nd inv   1st inv   1st inv

quality——   ———   ———   ———

root ———   ———   ———   ———

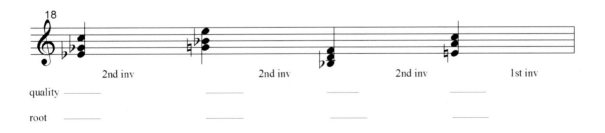

2nd inv   2nd inv   2nd inv   1st inv

quality ———   ———   ———   ———

root ———   ———   ———   ———

ist inv   2nd inv   2nd inv   1st inv

quality ———   ———   ———   ———

root ———   ———   ———   ———

Homework 22

I. Identify the pitches using their   II Rewrite the measure below in the next measure using the octava sign
pitch octave designation.

III. 1. Name the note AND 2. Notate and name its
enharmarmonic equivalent next to it

IV. Label the wholesteps (WS) and halfstep (HS) are in this scale. Identify the scale.

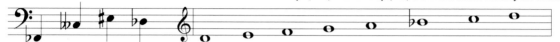

V.   Write the note BELOW   VI. Write the note ABOVE   VII.   What is the meter and meter type?
to make the given interval   to make the given interval   (compound duple, simple triple, etc.)

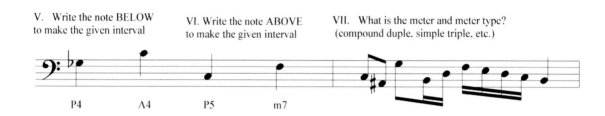

P4   A4   P5   m7

VIII. Invert the interval and label both   IX. Write out the following scales USING accidentals
                                                        c harmonic minor scale

X. What are the keys (major and minor)   XI. Notate the following notes in the specified keys
 for each of the following key signatures?   using accidentals NOT key signatures

1. subdominant in F major   2. mediant in g minor

XII. Beam the notes correctly for the given meter. Write in the counts.

XIII. Identify the following chords (M, m, A, d)

XIV. Identify the Roman number for each chord in the given key (I, V, vi, etc.).

C#: ___   Eb: ____   e: _____

XV. Musical elements

1. *D.C. al Fine* (what does it mean, what musical direction is it giving you?)

2. *D.S. al Fine* (what does it mean, what musical direction is it giving you?)

3. Draw the repeat sign.

4. What is the difference between meter, rhythm, measure, beat, and tempo?

5. What does *pianissimo* mean?

6. What does *ritardando* mean?

Answers to Chapter Exercises

Chapter 1
Exercise 1.3
What is the pitch octave designation?

E5

Exercise 1.4

A3   A3   A4   A4

Exercise 1.5

Identify these notes

D#   Fbb   Fb   B×

Exercise 1.6
Notate and name two enharmonic notes for the given note

A#   Bb   Cbb   Fb   E   D×   B   Cb   A×   F×   G   Abb

Chapter 2
Exercise 2.1
Is the meter in groups of 2, 3, or 4?   4

Exercise 2.2

Exercise 2.3
What gets the beat?

Exercise 2.4
How many beats?

Exercise 2.5
How many beats does each note get?

Exercise 2.6
Beam the notes.

Exercise 2.7
What is the meter classification?

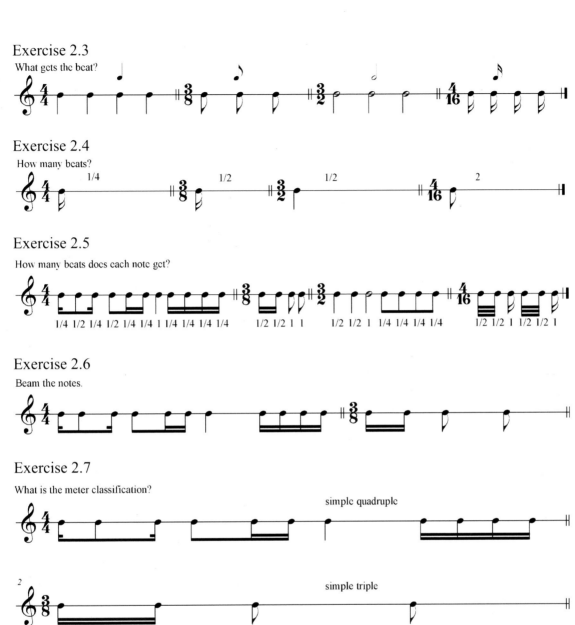

Exercise 2.8

Write in the counts.

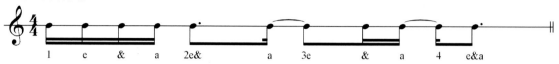

1   e   &   a   2e&   a   3e   &   a   4   e&a

Chapter 3
Exercise 3.1

What is the pitch octave designation for each note?

C6   D6   E6   G6   F3   E3   F3   G3   D3   G2

Exercise 3.2

Rewrite without ledger lines using the octava sign

Exercise 3.3

Rewrite in other staff using the octava sign

Chapter 4
Exercise 4.1

Simple or compound?

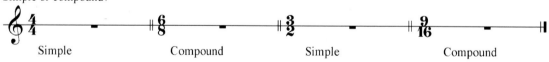

Simple   Compound   Simple   Compound

Exercise 4.2

How many beats per measure?

4   6/2 = 2   3   9/3 = 3

Exercise 4.3
What gets the beat?

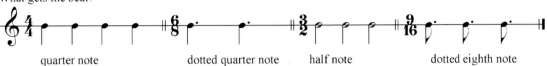

quarter note   dotted quarter note   half note   dotted eighth note

Exercise 4.4
Write in the counts.

1   2   3   456

Exercise 4.5
What is the meter classification?

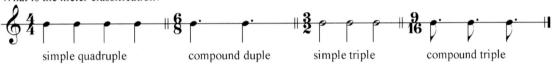

simple quadruple   compound duple   simple triple   compound triple

Exercise 4.6
How many beats?

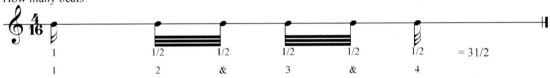

1   1/2   1/2   1/2   1/2   1/2   = 3 1/2
1   2   &   3   &   4

Exercise 4.7
How many beats?

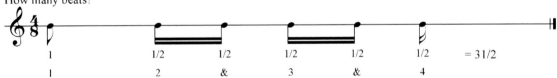

1   1/2   1/2   1/2   1/2   1/2   = 3 1/2
1   2   &   3   &   4

Chapter 5
Exercise 5.1
What gets the beat?

dotted half note   eighth note   dotted whole note   sixteenth note

Exercise 5.2
Write in the counts.

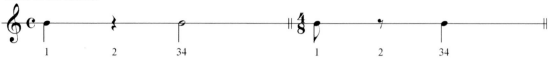

Exercise 5.3
Write in the counts.

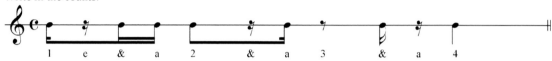

Exercise 5.4
Write in the counts.

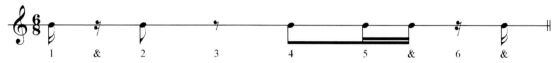

Exercise 5.5
Write in the counts.

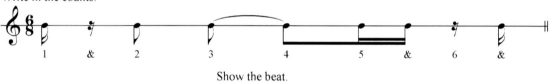

Show the beat.

Exercise 5.6
How many beats?   2/3 + 1/6 + 1/6 + 1/3 + 1/6 + 1/6 = 1 2/3

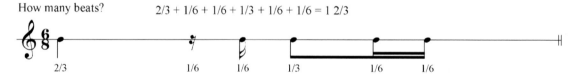

Exercise 5.7
Add one note to complete the measure.

Exercise 5.8
Insert barlines and write in the counts.

Chapter 6
Exercise 6.1

Exercise 6.2

Exercise 6.3
What is the tonic of E♭? What is the subdominant of E♭?   E♭ and A♭

Exercise 6.4
Notate a descending E major scale.

Chapter 7
Exercise 7.2
F C G D A E B
B E A D G C F

Exercise 7.3

Exercise 7.4

Exercise 7.5
What is the dominant of B♭? F

Chapter 8
Exercise 8.1

Exercise 8.3

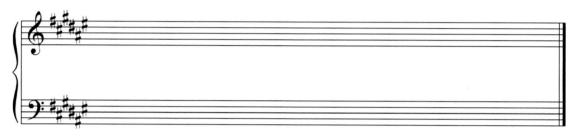

Exercise 8.4

What is the key?   c♯ minor

Chapter 9
Exercise 9.1

Exercise 9.2

Exercise 9.3

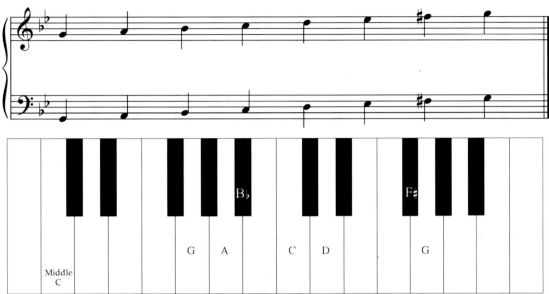

Exercise 9.4

Exercise 9.6

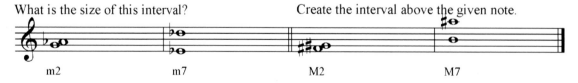

Chapter 10
Exercise 10.1

What is the size of this interval?

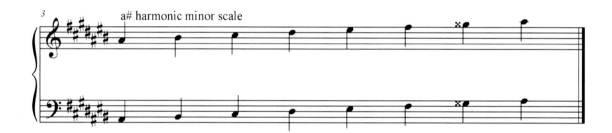

Exercise 10.2

What is the size of this interval?   Create the interval above the given note.

Exercise 10.3

What is the size of this interval?   Create the interval above the given note.

m2   m7   M2   M7

Exercise 10.4

What is the size of this interval?   Create the interval above the given note.

M3   m3   M3   m3

Exercise 10.5

What is the size of this interval?   Create the interval above the given note.

A3   M3   M3   d3

Exercise 10.6

What is the size of this interval?   Create the interval above the given note.

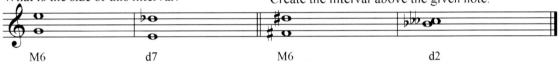

M6   d7   M6   d2

Exercise 10.7

What is the size of this interval?   Create the interval above the given note.

A8   AU   P8   PU

Exercise 10.8

Create the interval above the given note.   Invert this interval and identify the resultant interval.

m3   M7   m7   M2   A6   d3

Exercise 10.9

Create the interval above the given note.   Invert this interval and identify the resultant interval.

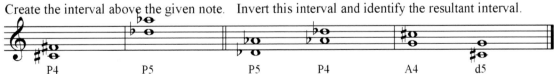

P4   P5   P5   P4   A4   d5

Exercise 10.10

Create the interval above the given note.   Invert this interval and identify the resultant interval.

A2   d5   M6   m3   m7   M2

Exercise 10.11

What is the size of the interval?.   Create this interval.

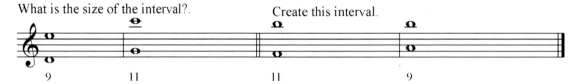

Exercise 10.12

What is this interval?.   Create this interval.

Chapter 11

Exercise 11. 1

Exercise 11. 2

Create a triad.

Exercise 11. 3

Create a triad.

Exercise 11. 4

Change each chord as indicated.

Exercise 11. 6

Notate all the white note triads as indicated.

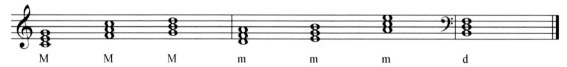

Exercise 11. 7

| Notate a triad above the root. | Notate chord, given note is the third. | Notate chord, given note is the fifth. |

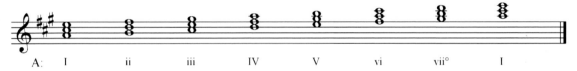

Exercise 11. 8

| Notate a M triad above the root | Notate m chord, given note is the third. | Notate d chord, given note is the fifth. |

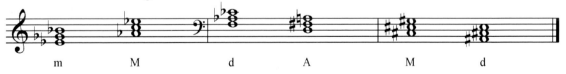

Chapter 12

Exercise 12.1

Label harmonized A Major scale with Roman Numerals

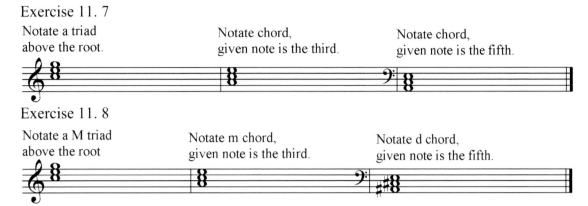

A: I   ii   iii   IV   V   vi   vii°   I

Exercise 12.2

Notate the primary triads in the key of B major and D♭ major.

B: I   IV   V   D♭ I   IV   V

Exercise 12.3

Assume the first chord to be tonic. What is the chord quality and roman numeral of the second chord?

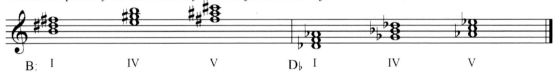

E: I   vi, m   F:I   IV, M   d: i   iv, m

Exercise 12.4

Create the chords on the given root.

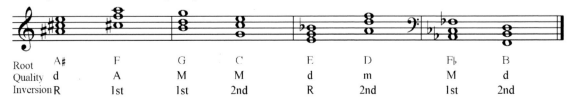

m   M   d   A   M   d

Exercise 12.5

Identify the root, the chord quality, and the inversion.

Root	A♯	F	G	C	E	D	F♭	B
Quality	d	A	M	M	d	m	M	d
Inversion	R	1st	1st	2nd	R	2nd	1st	2nd